DANCING
THROUGH
LIFE IN
A PAIR OF
BROKEN
HEELS

DANCING THROUGH LIFE IN A PAIR OF BROKEN HEELS

Extremely Short Stories for the Totally Stressed

Written by Mickey Guisewite
Illustrated by Cathy Guisewite

BANTAM BOOKS
NEW YORK · TORONTO · LONDON · SYDNEY · AUCKLAND

DANCING THROUGH LIFE IN A PAIR OF BROKEN HEELS

A Bantam Book /July 1993

Book design by Richard Oriolo

Library of Congress Cataloging-in-Publication Data
Guisewite, Mickey.
    Dancing through life in a pair of broken heels : extremely
short stories for the totally stressed / written by Mickey
Guisewite ; illustrated by Cathy Guisewite.
        p.   cm.
    ISBN 0-553-09190-5
    I. Guisewite, Cathy.   II. Title.
PN6727.G77D36   1993
814'.54—dc20   93-14646
                                                    CIP

Published simultaneously in the United States and Canada

Bantam Books are published by Bantam Books, a division of
Bantam Doubleday Dell Publishing Group, Inc. Its trademark,
consisting of the words "Bantam Books" and the portrayal of a
rooster, is Registered in U.S. Patent and Trademark Office and
in other countries. Marca Registrada. Bantam Books, 1540
Broadway, New York, New York 10036.

PRINTED IN THE UNITED STATES OF AMERICA

RRC   0 9 8 7 6 5 4 3

To Mom, Dad, and John,
my human support hose.

M.G.

CONTENTS

CONTENTS

ACKNOWLEDGMENTS

Had I not spent a total of three hundred and thirty-seven hours on the phone with my sisters Mary Anne and Cathy, my editor Barbara Alpert, my agent Cullen Stanley, and my very closest girlfriends, I would have spent the last seven months alone in a little room seeking moral support from my word processor. For the constant inspiration and encouragement, the friendship and advice, I thank you all. My indebtedness to you comes close to what I owe the phone company.

FOREWORD
by Cathy Guisewite

My professional respect for Mickey began the day she called from a business trip and begged me to Federal Express my black sling-back pumps to her hotel room because none of the six pairs of black shoes she'd taken on her two day trip was quite right for her big meeting. Every older sister hopes she's been something of a role model . . . but Mickey's astounding ability to focus on the completely mundane while her entire career teetered on the brink impressed even me.

If I was touched by the shoe incident, I was moved to tears the day she called me from a pay phone in the ladies' room of a restaurant to ask what I thought her fiancé might have meant when he said she looked nice.

This is a woman who knows how to obsess. This is a woman whose first act as a new bride was to have her own phone line installed so she could continue to get hourly, private, long-distance opinions on what she should wear if her husband asked her out to the movies. This is a woman who can look life right in the eye and know with all her heart that all aspects of it would be going better if only she'd gotten the slightly more taupey shade of eyeshadow.

In the last ten of the seventeen years I've been writing the CATHY™ comic strip, Mickey's the only person I've ever read my jokes to before drawing them, let alone pleaded with to help me make them actually contain some humor. Time and time again, she's been willing to tap into her own personal spectrum of humiliating moments to embellish, reinforce, or forbid me from publishing the comic strip I was about to create.

In *Dancing Through Life in a Pair of Broken Heels,* Mickey gives us forty-one chances to take a little break from our own angst and enjoy some of hers. Why does the world-famous hairstylist turn into a deranged hack when he gets to her? Why can't there be one uniform code for secret blabbing among women? Why does "quality time with families" begin at 6:30 P.M. when everyone's ready to strangle each other? How is it that the same man who hates to hear a story repeated once has been mesmerized by one golf video for the last three years? Why isn't there a law forbidding us to read *Cosmopolitan* magazine before speaking to a member of the opposite sex?

Mickey helps us laugh at things we've been through and, maybe more important, helps us laugh at things we don't even know we're going through: the little aggravations . . . the big frustrations . . . and all the miscellaneous embarrassments that pile up in our brains and sit there slowly sapping the energy we might use to accomplish something.

Although she's younger, thinner, cuter, and married to a perfect man, she has managed to maintain the perfect balance between confident indignance and insecure, guilt-ridden paranoia that I have strived for all my life. Looking at her work, I like to feel it will be clear who inspired her—that there's one special woman in her life who's nurtured not only the optimistically doomed outlook, but the compelling need to maintain a sense of humor about it.

Suffice it to say, Mickey and I grew up with the same mother.

TO LOVE, HONOR, AND BLAB EVERYTHING YOU KNOW

I am seated across from my best girlfriend and confidante of fifteen years.

"You know that thing I told you the other day?" I say, leaning in so no one else in the restaurant will hear.

"What thing?"

"You know, the thing about my pants splitting two

seconds before I had to stand up and give that presentation."

"Oh, yeah," she says, starting to snicker.

"How embarrassing. Boy, I'm just glad you're the only one who knows," I say, reconfirming our vow of secrecy.

"Oh, um—"

"I mean, you didn't tell anyone, did you?"

"Well, no. Except of course for Ted."

I stare at my friend incredulously. "Ted? You told Ted?!"

"Ted's my husband. I tell Ted everything."

Everything? Everything?! Everything I've told her since the day they got married a year ago? Is that the everything she means?

My mind races, conjuring up all the secrets I've told my friend in the last twelve months: the-nervous-breakdown-in-front-of-my-boss-over-the-miserable-raise episode; the-top-half-of-my-jumpsuit-in-the-toilet-at-the-fancy-restaurant incident; the wandering-shoulder-pad-as-accidental-third-breast-at-the-cocktail-party embarrassment.

I can feel my face starting to turn red. "Everything?"

"Oh, come on. He thought the pants ripping thing was almost as funny as your ill-fated bikini waxing before your romantic week in Bermuda."

"That?!" I gasp. "You told him that?! But you were only dating Ted a week when I told you that!"

"Well, of course I didn't tell him then," she says, rolling her eyes at me. "We barely knew each other then. I told him right after the in-flight diarrhea episode."

I'm overcome with nausea, not unlike the queasy sensation Princess Diana must have felt when the secretly taped phone conversations with her boyfriend were broadcast around the world. "The in-flight diarrhea episode?! We swore the two of us would be the only people in the world who would ever know about the in-flight diarrhea episode!"

"But Ted and I were living together then," she says matter-of-factly.

My mind speeds out of control, trying to remember every secret I've ever told my friend since the two of them moved in together, which apparently was the same day she felt obliged to begin blabbing all of my confidences to him.

"But even if it was okay to tell him about the in-flight diarrhea episode because you were living together, *it did not* make it okay for you to tell him about the ill-fated bikini wax."

"Why not?"

"That happened well before the two of you moved in," I say, getting more heated. "I mean, if you told him that, why not just go ahead and tell him about my liposuction?"

"Oh. Um, your liposuction—"

"But you weren't even dating Ted then! You were living with Alex!"

"Yes, but I'm in love with Ted now. How could I possibly have told Alex something but keep it from Ted?"

I sit staring at my friend, speechless. I had always thought that in the unwritten rules of female friendship, right beneath Rule Number One—A woman will not look better than her best friend at her best friend's wedding, was Rule Number Two—A woman will guard her friend's confidences with the same shroud of secrecy she guards her own hip and upper thigh measurements.

If my best friend didn't see it my way, what could I possibly expect from my other confidantes?

Lisa just moved in with Dennis. Did she manage to make it past the threshold before she spilled the beans about my Valentine's Day tantrum she swore would always be our little secret?

Kate's been out with Joel three times. Is she two dates away from blabbing about the week I spent Solarcaining my bright red breasts after a four-hour journey into the world of topless sunbathing?

And what about Janice? She just got divorced from Brian, who is now seeing Cynthia. Were my personal humiliations part of the divorce settlement along with the desk lamp and Barcalounger chair? Is Cynthia, a woman whom I've never even met, now telling everyone she knows about the time I made the unfortunate choice of eating two packages of Metamucil crackers five hours before a date?

"So what's going on with you?" my friend says, changing the subject.

"Nothing. You?"

"Not much."

I look at her and think about how the bond between a man and a woman changes the bond between two women forever. I think about how we weep uncontrollably as we watch our sisters standing at the altar. Tears of joy? Hardly. I think it's because, beyond a doubt, we know we've just watched our secrets go marching down the aisle.

THE 59.9-MINUTE GOURMET

I t says it right there on the cover of the book: "Dozens of meals you can cook in under an hour." Beneath the title stands the book's author with a complete gourmet feast she has apparently prepared in 59.9 minutes or less: Chicken Provençal, Sautéed Spinach, Arugula and Red Leaf Salad, and Apple Tartlets. All in under an hour?

But something is seriously missing here. I inspect the cover closely to check for traces of the author's extra six sets of arms I'm sure have been airbrushed out of the photo.

So I'm leery. But at the same time I can't help being impressed. The food looks great. But the author looks even better. She's confident. Neatly dressed. Her makeup is perfectly applied, and she has no Chicken Provençal grease stains on her pretty mauve top and skirt.

I like this woman. I want to be able to whip up impromptu five-course dinners with exotic-sounding dishes for family and friends like she does. I want to own her mauve outfit and matching mauve lipstick. I grab the book, shell out my $23.00, and speed home, ready to embark on my life as a 59.9-minute-or-less gourmet.

After spending a few minutes at home paging through the book, I'm even more impressed with its author. Not only has she created dozens of menus complete with appetizer, soup or salad, main course, and dessert, she's categorized them into the appropriate seasons in which they are to be served. Who would have known that Roast Leg of Lamb with Mustard Glaze, Parsnip Purée, Sautéed Morels, Braised Red Cabbage, and Chocolate Hazelnut Soufflé are the perfect thing to serve on a late November day?

Not me. Even though it's only June fourteenth, I decide to invite three friends over for the Roast Leg of Lamb menu, hoping they won't notice my seasonal faux pas.

They don't. Possibly because they never get a chance to taste it. Possibly because I'm never able to locate all the ingredients, let alone cook them by the time my guests arrive. It's all kind of a blur to me now, but my debut as a 59.9-minute-or-less gourmet went something like this:

9:00 A.M. SATURDAY MORNING: CALL GUESTS: "I know it's kind of last minute, but I was wondering if you'd like to pop over for some Roast Leg of Lamb tonight?" (I try posing the invitation in the same casual, breezy manner I imagine the author would.)

All politely accept. All politely refrain from confronting me with the roast lamb in June issue.

10:00 A.M.–12:00 NOON: SEARCH FOR A MAUVE OUTFIT AND MATCHING LIPSTICK: I have become obsessed with this outfit and lipstick combo. I become even more obsessed when I find it no longer exists. Of course, I'm sure it did exist back when the author found it. Back in February when the department stores were stocked with soft summer pastels. But now all I see are rack after rack of autumn greens and reds and golds. (Which, come to think of it, would probably match the Roast Leg of Lamb and Braised Red Cabbage better.)

I leave the mall empty-handed except for the $100.00 skin-care system the lady at the makeup counter talks me into.

12:00–4:00 P.M. SATURDAY: SEARCH CITY FOR FOODS THE A & P DOESN'T SELL: Like the main course, for example. Or balsamic vinegar. Or freshly grated nutmeg. Or fresh thyme. Or morel mushrooms, which I never do locate because they are out of season.

7

By the time my food gathering is complete, I've put forty-three miles on my car and am beginning to compose a curt letter in my head to the author:

Dear Lady with the Nonexistent Mauve Outfit,
    Might you have noted in your cookbook that some of the ingredients necessary for the Roast Leg of Lamb dinner (that I most certainly would never think of preparing in June but am only now finding time to write to you about) are just a tad bit hard to find?

4:00 P.M. SATURDAY: BEGIN PREPARING 59.9-MINUTE-OR-LESS MEAL.

4:01 P.M. SATURDAY: CALL MOTHER: "Mom, I'm having friends over for a five-course roast lamb dinner in an hour and a half. What am I supposed to do?"

"Roast lamb, sweetie? Why don't you just whip up something summery and light like salad, grilled chicken, green beans, and ice cream for dessert?"

"Muh-thrrrr—"

"Do you want me to come over?"

Leave it to my mother to expose my roast lamb in June blunder. I'm totally annoyed. "No, that's okay."

4:15–5:15 P.M. SATURDAY:

Dear Lady with the Mauve Outfit I Don't Much Care for Anymore,
    Thank you very much for neglecting to note until the middle of your stupid recipe that I would need to buy a $145.00 appliance to complete it.

• • •

This is what I think to myself as I'm frantically driving around trying to locate the food processor needed to make both the Parsnip Purée and Hazelnut Soufflé.

5:15–6:15 P.M. SATURDAY: My guests are due in forty-five minutes. I slice. I dice. I chop. I peel. I race around the kitchen trying to accomplish in forty-five minutes what anyone else knows should take six hours.

By 5:55 P.M. all I've managed to do is spray liquefied parsnips all over my kitchen.

I slam the cookbook shut. There she is with that condescending look on her face, smugly grinning at me: "I can whip up a Roast Leg of Lamb with Mustard Glaze, Parsnip Purée, Sautéed Morels, Braised Red Cabbage, and Chocolate Hazelnut Soufflé in under an hour, and you can't."

I think she's sticking out her tongue at me. I think they airbrushed it out along with her extra six sets of arms.

MATING CALL OF
THE SEVEN UNDER PAR

Some women search the pages of *Elle* and *Vogue*, studying fashions that supposedly will make them more attractive to men.

Some women pore over the Victoria's Secret catalogue, studying lingerie styles that allegedly will make them more seductive to men.

Some women read self-help book after self-help book, studying advice that apparently will make them more compatible with men.

Me? I study the Nick Faldo tape.

Nick Faldo, a man in bright green polyester golf pants.

Nick Faldo, the man with the perfect swing.

Nick Faldo, who after winning the 1987 British Open, unfortunately chose to create a seventy-five minute golf video, which still keeps the man in my life mesmerized after four hundred and seventy-eight viewings.

Okay. I'll come right out and say it. I'm jealous of the guy.

"George Burns was sitting at the table next to me!" I say excitedly.

"Yeah," he replies, "you mentioned that yesterday."

I would like to point out that the man who is not interested in hearing a second time about how one of the greatest Hollywood legends actually tapped his cigar in my direction, has replayed Nick Faldo's electrifying story about how it took him two years to perfect his grip no fewer than six hundred times.

"How would you like to go to the ballet tonight?" I ask, hoping to pique his interest.

"I've seen the ballet."

"Which ballet?"

"I don't know. *The* ballet."

Again, I must interject that the man who has just grouped five hundred years' worth of dance into one nameless ballet has been forced to replace his Nick Faldo tape with a new one because the "Technique of Bunker Play" section is so worn out.

He hangs on Nick's every word. Watches his every move. Imitates his every gesture.

"Why do you have a golf club stuck between your legs?" I ask while passing through the family room.

"It's one of Nick's drills. It helps keep my torso in line. See?"

No, I really don't see at all. But I say, "Oh, yes," as encouragingly as I'm sure Nick would if he were here.

Five minutes later I pass through the room again. "Why do you have a bath towel stuffed under your armpits?"

"It's a practice drill Nick does to get his body and arms into position."

"Nice!" I chime.

The next time I walk by the family room he's waving my ten-year-old niece's beach ball around in the air. I don't even ask. I'm only thankful Mr. Faldo doesn't subject his viewers to a concentration drill where he runs barefoot over hot coals, or I'd be ordering new carpet right now.

I find myself simultaneously fascinated and repulsed by Nick Faldo. What is it about this man? How is he able to hold the entire male population spellbound in a way that has eluded me for the last thirty-two years?

Could it be his magnetic personality, I wonder while shoving the tape into the VCR.

"Stay down and believe the loft of the club will get the ball airborne . . ." "Be aggressive. Hit firmly through . . ." "Let's talk a little about putting, shall we. . . ."

I wake up twenty-five minutes later, convinced that we can eliminate personality as a factor. No, it must be something else, like perhaps Nick's spectacular sense of personal style.

I fast-forward the tape and note that he wears the same pair of bright green polyester golf pants and white T-shirt throughout the entire tape. The towel he shoves under his armpits doesn't even match his outfit.

Then I fast-forward to the end of the tape and watch a montage of Nick in his moment of glory: Nick in slow motion as he sinks the final putt. Nick in slow motion with the British Open trophy high above his head. Nick in slow motion waving at his cheering, adoring fans.

It's as though he's saying, "Stick with me. Stick with me through seven thousand more viewings and all this could be yours."

I quickly flip the remote and sit in helpless silence. How can one woman's seductive powers possibly compete with that?

A MUZZLE FOR
TABLE THREE, PLEASE

I am sitting across from her. The woman I worship and adore. The most beautiful woman I've ever known. The most charming, caring, and nurturing person in the world. The only person I know who would drop whatever she was doing to rush to my aid. The only person in the world who truly understands me.

Thirty-two years of emotion bottled up inside me, and this is what comes out:

"For God's sake, Mother, you've been staring at the menu for five minutes! Would you make up your mind already?!"

No. That's not what I meant to say at all. I meant to say something pleasant, something like—

"Sweetie, you seem tense today," she pipes up. "Are you and Mark still having that little problem?"

The Mark thing. How can I possibly be pleasant when she insists on talking about the Mark thing? Does she think of nothing else but the Mark thing? Must we dwell on the Mark thing? Fifty years from now when I open my mailbox, will I still be getting pointers and tips and Dear Abby clippings on how to deal with the Mark thing?

Of course, four months ago, when it was all I thought about day and night, I opened up and told her about the Mark thing. It was during one of those spontaneous moments while we were sitting in her kitchen that I not only told her about the Mark thing, I confessed every other anxiety in my life.

The advice she gave me helped with the Mark thing. I should tell her that. I should tell her how much she—

"You know, the other day Dear Abby did a little piece that might help you with the Mark—"

"Mom, that was over four months ago!" I snap.

Unbelievable. There I go again. She's only expressing her motherly concern and I—

"Oh, sweetie, look at that cute little baby," my mother says, looking over my shoulder.

I turn around to look.

Baby? Which baby? Everywhere I look there are babies. Table after table of babies. A sea of babies. Babies and mommies and adoring grandmothers treating them to lunch.

It seems we're the only babyless table in the entire restaurant. Of course, if I had my own cute little baby right now, my mother wouldn't be having to make goofy faces at babies halfway across the restaurant.

Why don't I have a cute little baby? Isn't that what she's really insinuating? Isn't that what she means?

"Cute," I say flatly.

But there's so much I want to ask her about having a baby. I have so many reservations. So many conflicting feelings. Did she have them too? She gave up a promising career to stay at home and have babies. How did she know that was what she wanted? Does she have any regrets? Wouldn't this be the perfect time to have a grown-up, woman-to-woman conversation about motherhood and lifelong goals and personal fulfillment and—

"So, how'd your big meeting go?" my mother asks, changing the subject.

The rich mother–daughter moment I'm having in my brain is put on hold.

"Fine," I say, growing more tense.

Fine? Is that all? Why not tell the truth? Why not say, "You wouldn't believe it, Mom. It was the worst meeting of my entire life. The client insisted we use him as the spokesperson for his commercial. We tried to talk him out of it. He wouldn't let up. So we went ahead and shot the commercial with him as spokesperson. And so yesterday in the meeting when we showed him the commercial for the first time, do you know what he said? He told us we made him look fat, which is sort of hard not to do when you're dealing with someone who has a seventy-three-inch waistline. And now we have to reshoot him again next week and somehow make him look like Patrick Swayze . . ." Instead, all I have to say is "Fine."

The more we talk, the less I have to say. She asks me if I need help getting ready for the party I'm having next week. I'm offended that she doesn't think I can handle it myself.

She tells me my hair looks nice, which I take as a complete insult, assuming that what she really means is that today is an exception to all other days.

The warm, compassionate thoughts that four minutes ago were right on the tip of my tongue are now being shoved to the back of my brain. Mean-spirited remarks are stampeding forward. Maybe it's better to sit quietly and say nothing at all. I won't even open my mouth for the split second it would take to insert a piece of bread, in case some terrible comment jumps out.

The silence is broken when the waitress comes to take our order.

"What'll you have today?"

The woman I worship and adore, the most beautiful woman I've ever known, the most charming, caring, and nurturing person in the world, the only person I know who would drop whatever she was doing to rush to my aid, the only person in the world who truly understands me, has made up her mind.

"I'll have soup and a salad."

But now I don't know what I want. I frantically search the menu and try to decide.

It's moments like the one we're having today that I must try to remember. Someday I hope to be sitting in a restaurant across from my own daughter. And when she says, "For God's sake, Mother, would you hurry up and make up your mind already?!" I'll know exactly what she means.

I THINK, THEREFORE
I AM FAT

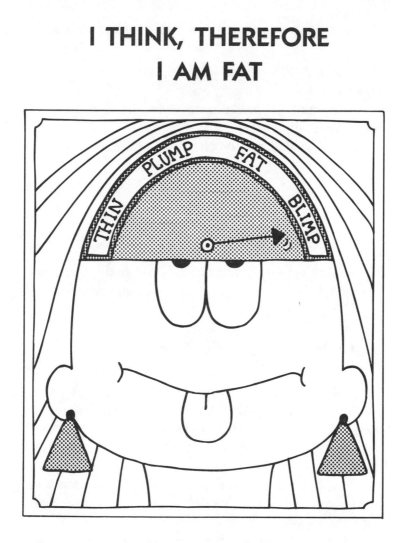

The reason men will never understand women's
weight anxiety is because men have never had to
get on the same scale we do: The one that is in our
brains.

The one that tells us every morning that we're fat.
The one that reminds us all day long that we're fat.

The one that continually depresses us because it says we're fat.

The one that makes us overeat because, what the heck, we're already fat.

The one that makes the following daily scenarios inevitable:

DAY ONE

HIM: Weighs self and notes two-pound weight loss. Proceeds to eat huge stack of pancakes and go about his day.

ME: Before I even get out of bed, I hear the scale in my brain telling me that today I am fat.

I stagger into the shower. Is it my imagination, or are the fat cells causing the water to ricochet off my body? Is my mind playing tricks on me, or did the bath towel somehow shrink overnight so that the ends barely meet?

Yes, I am fat. Incredibly fat. Fatter than I've ever been in my whole life. I waddle into the bedroom and open the closet.

"I am so fat today," I announce to all of my clothes.

But can I possibly be as fat as I feel? I lumber back into the bathroom to consult the scale. It tells me that in fact, I have lost two pounds. Two pounds? I've lost two pounds?!

I race back to my closet to give my clothes an update. But now it's too late. They've already gotten the news that I am fat today, and have apparently broadcast it to my lingerie drawer.

"But I lost two pounds!" I scream at my pantyhose, which only yesterday were baggy and now form a tourniquet flab line around my middle.

"But I lost two pounds!" I shriek at my skirt as I try to force the zipper up over my left thigh.

"But I lost two pounds!" I wail at my jacket that refuses to close in front.

Disgusted and demoralized, I go into the kitchen, eat a stack of pancakes, and then attempt to squeeze myself into the front seat of my car. I stop once for a new pair of pantyhose, once for a breakfast burrito, once for a side of hash browns, and once for a box of doughnuts that would have been for my co-workers had I not personally needed the extra energy to haul my immense body fifty feet from my parking space to the office door.

DAY TWO

HIM: Weighs self and notes four-pound weight gain. Proceeds to eat huge stack of pancakes and go about his day.

ME: I awaken to hear the scale in my brain telling me that today I am thin. Hallelujah! A miracle has occurred.

I bounce out of bed and leap into the shower, immediately noting how the water glides down my flat stomach and slender thighs.

Moments later I leap out of the shower and jump on

the scale for confirmation. Two seconds later I jump off the scale. Apparently the force with which I leapt has caused the scale to measure my weight three pounds too high.

Hanging on to the towel rack, I gingerly step back on the scale. Apparently eight years' worth of lingering hair spray particles have made the air extremely dense, therefore adding four more pounds to my true weight.

I grab the scale and take it into the hallway. The floor is so uneven, it tips the scale to the right five pounds.

I carry the scale into the bedroom. But the carpeting is like a little trampoline that shoots my weight up not five, but six pounds.

I race to the closet and frantically attempt to slip into a skirt and blouse before news of the phony excess pounds reaches the closet. But I'm too late.

"But my brain scale says I'm thin!" I scream at my brand-new pantyhose, which explode at the sight of my enormous toe.

"But my brain scale says I'm thin!" I shriek at my skirt while trying to maneuver it over my hips.

"But my brain scale says I'm thin!" I wail at my blouse as the center button pops.

I can feel my face turning red with anger. Once again, I've been betrayed. If my brain scale insisted on making me feel fat when I actually wasn't, why don't I believe it now and insist that I am thin, no matter what the bathroom scale says? Must I always believe the scale that says I'm the fattest?

Enraged, I trundle into the kitchen and eat two stacks of pancakes—one because I'm already fat, and one because frankly all the confusion has made me kind of hungry.

DAY THREE

HIM: Searches bathroom for scale. Sees miscellaneous scale parts strewn about floor. Follows numbers, pointer, coils, and spring down hallway leading to me lying in a depressed stupor on the bed.
HIM: What's the matter?
ME: I am so fat.
HIM: You don't look fat.
ME: I gained ten pounds.
HIM: How would you know? The scale's broken.
ME: Believe me, I know.
HIM: Aw, c'mon. It's all in your head.

No kidding. I couldn't have put it better myself.

BLITHERING
BY THE RULES

I don't want to hear about it. I don't want to think about it. I don't want to talk about it. And yet, after my friend Carol and I have been together for just four minutes, I can see that look in her eyes. And, being an obliging friend, I say those three little words nearly every woman I know right now longs to hear: "How's the baby?"

"The baby? Oh, I just took the cutest pictures of her," she says, whipping out a package of photos. "Doesn't she have the most precious face you've ever seen?"

"Oh yes, precious," I say. But I can't help thinking how much more expressive my own little Joey's face is. Always bright. Always smiling. Never a tear.

"Here she is clapping her hands. The doctor says she's incredibly coordinated for her age."

"Wow," I say. But I can't help thinking how much more impressive it is that my little Joey was able to catch a ball in mid-air at age five months.

"And here's Madeline eating her birthday cake. She kind of missed her mouth."

Of course I can't help thinking how much more amusing my little Joey's experiences with food have been. . . . Like the time when, five minutes before guests were to arrive, I had to try and make the tail end of my salmon mousse look like a necktie, because my little Joey had eaten the head. Or the time he ate a container of Kentucky Fried Chicken including the box and receipt, but demonstrated extraordinary willpower by leaving the buttermilk biscuits completely untouched.

But I restrain myself. I say nothing. At age thirty-two I have no children to go on and on about. But I do have a dog.

And soon enough I will have my chance to go on and on about him, because we are operating on a basic principle of female friendship here: the one that guarantees equal time to blither on about the obsessions of our lives.

And so I sit patiently waiting for my turn. I lend a

sympathetic ear as my friend tells me about Madeline's little problem of roaming the house like a twenty-two-pound human vacuum cleaner, digesting every bug and hair ball that comes into her path. Why? Because soon I'll be describing Joey's little problem of being unable to greet visitors without torpedoing his six-inch nose directly into their crotches.

I politely wade through thirty-six nearly identical photos of her little Madeline throwing a tantrum on Santa's lap. Why? Because soon my friend will be politely wading through thirty-six nearly identical photos of my little Joey mutilating his Christmas reindeer antlers.

I thoughtfully nod my head up and down and grunt in the appropriate places as my friend describes the scene her daughter makes when she's dropped off at day care each morning. Why? Because soon she'll be doing the same for me when I describe the cute way my Joey sits completely depressed in the coat closet each morning to protest my leaving him.

I chuckle along as she— Wait a minute. According to the equal-time-for-blithering rule, we're heading into some serious overtime on the endearing little Madeline stories. I discreetly check my watch and note that forty-five minutes into our conversation, there has been no mention of my little Joey.

Has motherhood completely obliterated her memory of the equal time rule that has been one of the hallmarks of our friendship for fifteen years? Is my one-year-old somehow less important than her one-year-old because mine has four legs and hers has two? And more important, could her purse possibly accommodate any more photographs than the seventy-five I've already seen?

Just as I find myself drifting into a coma, I hear the word *Joey*.

"Joey?" I ask, snapping to attention.

"I was just saying how cute it is when our next door neighbor's son Joey plays with Madeline. Here, I've got some pictures of them in my purse . . ."

Oh for crying out loud, who cares! Is it not enough that I've pleasantly sat through fifty minutes of Madeline anecdotes and photos? Must I now fawn over another one-year-old I don't even know to prove I'm a loyal friend? Will the conversation **ever** turn to my Joey? The cute Joey? The Joey with hair??

And even if it does, do I care to tell her? Would my friend think I'm completely crazy for believing that a dog capable of eating rotting pot roast remains out of the garbage somehow prefers his dog food warmed in the microwave? Would she think I'm absolutely nuts for insisting he was merely demonstrating his highly cultivated taste in footwear when he chose to destroy my Italian designer boots instead of the $12.00 sneakers sitting right next to them?

Certainly no more of a nut than I think she is for dreaming that when her daughter bangs aimlessly on their piano, the child is well on her way to becoming the next Vladimir Horowitz.

It's becoming quite clear to me that while motherhood may be universal, talking about it does not transcend species. And so if she ever happens to ask about my Joey, I won't even tell her. I'll just nod and say fine and that will be the—

"So, how's Joey?"

"Joey? . . . My Joey?"

"Yeah. How's your dog?"

Well, maybe just one picture . . . No, two . . . No, she must see all ninety-seven photos, and hear the fascinating anecdote that accompanies each.

I hear a stifled yawn. Almost like magic, her eyes glaze over, and I know she's my captive audience for the next sixty minutes. But then, isn't that what friends are for?

LAMINATED CORNFLAKES
AND OTHER PROBLEMS

In life we're always being told not to take the easy way out. Some of us have perfected this bit of wisdom into an art form.

The easy way out of standing in line for three hours at the Secretary of State's office the day your plates expire would have been to just send in the renewal application you got in the mail two months ago.

The easy way out of trying to remove the corn-flakes that are now sealed to the bottom of your cereal bowl would have been to just rinse the bowl two days ago, as soon as you'd finished eating.

The easy way out of the relationship would have been to end it the night of your first date, when you determined you did not like his hair, personality, physical appearance, taste in clothing, or hobbies, instead of now, six months later, when you're scheduled to move in together next week.

I wish I had taken the easy way out. Seven months ago I had the chance. That was when I received the gift from my friend. It was a little clock she had found.

A little clock that, back then, would've required a little thank-you note. A little thank-you note I somehow never sent.

The first two weeks I didn't send the note, I blame on lack of time. I was busy at work, busy at home, busy with friends. Too busy to write a note as thoughtful as my friend's gift.

From that point on, however, I found that as my guilt grew for having sent no note, so did my system for assessing blame.

My family was the first to blame. They had no problem that could be included as an excuse in the note I planned to write a month after the fact:

"Dear Anne,
    Sorry I haven't written to thank you for the beautiful clock, but things have been sort of hectic

around here with Uncle Ray's emergency gallblad-
der surgery and all."

No such luck. I come from very healthy stock. It
was time to shift blame to someone I could count on to
be at fault, like our Federal Government:

"Dear Anne,
     Well, thanks to the postal service, I only today
received your wonderful clock that I see was post-
marked three months ago. Can you believe it?"

No, I couldn't either. Even in my slightly deluded
state, this excuse seemed pretty flimsy.
     By month four, I couldn't bear to look at the clock
anymore, or hear its incessant ticking. I removed it from
the mantel and stuffed it in the closet. Tick, tick, tick.
Tick, tick, tick. I flung open the closet door at 3:00 A.M.
and yanked out the battery.
     I was agitated. I was annoyed. I was beginning to
feel victimized by my friend's thoughtfulness. Yes, *she*
was to blame for my misery. Had she sent me no gift at
all, I wouldn't have this obligation hanging over my
head. I wouldn't get a knot in my stomach every time I
looked at a clock. I would still be wearing a watch.
     Months five and six left me feeling guilty and
ashamed that I could ever feel this way about my friend.
After all, we'd shared a lot over the years. If and when
she ever called me again, I'd clear the whole matter up:

HER: How do you like the clock I sent?
ME: What clock?

It is now seven months later. Fortunately, my friend has never called, and I've moved past the point of feeling reduced to lying to her.

Now I blame a greeting card industry that has every type of card imaginable except belated thank-you notes for clocks. I blame Emily Post for writing a thousand-page etiquette manual that offers no advice for my particular problem.

But mostly, I find myself looking toward Christmas. Is it only three months away? I've decided I will search the city for a special gift for my friend, and enclose a lengthy letter in my Christmas card to her . . . Or in my Valentine's Day card to her . . . Or in my birthday card to her in April . . .

There's plenty of time. I should know. I have a clock.

NAKED AT THE OFFICE

I am seated behind my desk wearing my gray power suit. The one with shoulder pads that make me look like a linebacker. The one I always wear when I mean business.

He is seated across from me. Bob, the co-worker who four weeks ago begged me to write a proposal for a prospective client for him because he was too busy. Bob, the colleague who left every night at 6:00 while I stayed late creating a masterpiece the client would love. Bob, who when the business pitch was over and we got the account, took complete credit for my work and now is on the brink of a promotion.

Bob, whose mouth I'd like to pry open right now so I can cram my shoulder pads down his throat—but I'm not going to, because I subscribe to *Working Woman* magazine and I know that the way to handle confrontations in the workplace is to remain cool and confident and strictly professional at all times.

I open my mouth to give my big speech, eight words of which I'm able to deliver coolly, confidently, and strictly professionally before I feel a lump in my throat and tears welling up in my eyes.

"Bob, I want you to know how angry, (SNIFF SNIFF), how (SNIFF) angry (HEAVE) I (BLINK BLINK) am."

Five thousand articles on how to negotiate intelligently at the office. Eight years of attending effective-communication-skills seminars. Thirty-two years of pledging allegiance to a new generation of women who demand respect and equality at the workplace: all lost in the split second it has taken my Maybelline waterproof mascara to start streaming down my cheeks.

This can't be happening. It isn't happening. Maybe I only think I'm crying. After all, in *Working Woman*'s "Ten Ways to Effectively Handle a Conflict with a Coworker," sniffing and heaving appear nowhere on the list.

I open my mouth and begin the big speech all over again.

"Bob, I, (HEAVE), I, (SNIFF), I (SNORT)—"

I was right. I am not crying. No, I am blubbering. Blubbering like a five-year-old who just fell off her bike.

The more I try to compose myself, the worse it gets, until the man sitting across from me is only hearing every eighth syllable of my impassioned speech.

"How (HEAVE) self know (SOB SOB) cred (SNIFF) some (CHOKE) work (HEAVE HEAVE)?"

"Are you okay?"

Am I okay? No, I am not okay. I just asked how you can live with yourself knowing you took credit for someone else's work. *You're* supposed to be on the spot right now. Not me. *You're* supposed to feel humiliated and embarrassed. Not me. *You're* supposed to be the one who's dreading the moment this conversation is over and news of it spreads up and down the halls like wildfire. Not me. *You're* supposed to—

"Here, do you want a Kleenex?"

The truth is, I would like a Kleenex very much at this particular moment in my life. Because if I had a Kleenex right now I would not be using the right sleeve of my power suit as a three-hundred-dollar hanky.

But I will not accept a Kleenex. Accepting a Kleenex would be like waving a little white flag of surrender. I shake my head no.

"Uh, sorry. I didn't mean to upset you." He stands up and walks to the door.

Wait. Get back here, you miserable thief. I have an entire five-minute speech to deliver, four minutes and fifty-three seconds of which you haven't even heard.

I rehearsed it at home this morning. I fine-tuned it on the drive in to work. It is a textbook example of effective communication techniques at work, and I really would like for someone other than my dog and the guy in the passing lane to hear me use them.

The door clicks shut and he is gone.

I sit back and contemplate what I've accomplished today, which, aside from ruining a suit, is reinforcing the stereotype of the hysterical female. How can he possibly understand that though I may have looked, sounded, and acted hysterical, I was not hysterical? I was angry.

I was so angry that had I been a man, I might have yelled so loud that the people up and down the hall could clearly hear every word of my speech without plastering themselves to the other side of my door. I might have put my fist through the wall or thrown something.

But I would not have cried. Because men do not cry when they get angry. They may yell and scream and throw a temper tantrum, but when it's all said and done and they're paying to have the wall replastered, at least they can hang on to some small shred of dignity. At least they did not cry.

I fling the door open. "Bob, get back in here!" I shriek.

Twenty-six people pop their heads out of their offices.

Bob, Dave, and fifteen other men stare in my direction.

Ten women, including me, begin to weep.

AS MISSED
ON THE VCR

The year was 1983. Along with twenty-five million other Americans, I raced out to purchase a video camera and VCR, and began capturing my family on tape.

No moment was missed. And every one of them was just as gripping as the next.

SCENES FROM THANKSGIVING DAY 1983

SCENE ONE: We catch my mother in the kitchen preparing Thanksgiving dinner. She sticks the turkey in the oven. Four hours later she takes the turkey out of the oven. I document every action-packed moment, including a particularly dramatic one in which she drops the turkey baster on the floor and bends over to pick it up.

SCENE TWO: We all sit at the dining table eating the turkey dinner. With clever, witty repartee such as "Pass the salt," and "Sure, would you like the pepper, too?" I wonder if I should excuse myself and get Hollywood on the line. We're a regular sitcom family.

SCENE THREE: We see twenty-five minutes' worth of footage of eight people splayed motionless in the living room.

Well, I could go on and on. But you get the idea. And perhaps will understand why the very next day I ran out and rented my first movie.

Though no match for the heart-racing account of my father's Thanksgiving Alka-Seltzer episode, I thought *An Officer and a Gentleman* might provide some entertainment value.

I stood in a video store packed with people whose first home video experience must have been similar to my own, and began thinking what a great idea this movie rental concept was. For mere pennies of what it would cost to go to the movie theater, I could watch a film in the comfort of my own home.

I shelled out two bucks, raced home, flipped on the TV, and stuck the cassette in the—Wait. What's this I see? It's sweeps week, and every major network is having round-the-clock, week-long specials on sex!

Four days passed. I would have liked to watch *An Officer and a Gentleman,* but by then I'd spent nearly every moment in the office comparing notes on all the sex specials with my co-workers. If I didn't get some work done at home that night I'd become the subject of a sweeps week special entitled "How Talking About Sex All Day at the Office Got Me Fired From My Job."

It was now day six. I had redeemed myself at the office, and could have watched *An Officer and a Gentleman,* but frankly was so disgusted that I owed $16.00 in late fees for a film I hadn't even seen, I couldn't bear to stick it in the VCR. I shoved it in my briefcase to be returned the next day when I dropped off my dry cleaning.

A week later, when the only piece of clothing I owned that did not need to be dry-cleaned was a pocket hanky, I finally made my way to the video store.

"That'll be $42.00."

"$42.00?! For $42.00 I could buy it."

"Fine. Cash, check, or charge?"

"But I don't want to buy *An Officer and a Gentleman.* I now hate *An Officer and a Gentleman.*"

"Fine. Cash, check, or charge?"

I flung $42.00 at him and left empty-handed. While other moviegoers may have learned a lesson of love, decency, and responsibility, *An Officer and a Gentleman* taught me an entirely different lesson: Deposit paycheck first. Return movie second.

Certainly though, on many occasions since then, I've rented plenty of movies, plopped myself down on the couch, and haven't even gotten up to go to the bathroom until the end. For me, a typical movie night goes something like this:

1. Spend forty-five minutes at the video rental carefully selecting a film.
2. Stick cassette in player.
3. Push play button.
4. Wake up and stagger off to bed just as the final credits roll by on the screen.

The quality of the film is irrelevant. Its subject matter insignificant. Fellini and Spielberg alike are no match for sweat pants, a couch, and the comalike state caused by positioning my body horizontally on it.

If nothing else, this makes for some interesting post-film critical analysis:

FRIEND: Didn't you love the way *Citizen Kane* ends?
ME: Oh, yes. It was dark. Bold . . . Heavy.

Of course I'm merely referring to the typeface and point size they picked for the closing credits, but my friend enthusiastically nods her head in agreement.

Two years ago I could have watched *Godfather III* in a theater for $6.00. But judging from the mixed reviews, it just seemed like one of those films I should wait and see for half the price on video. To date, I've rented it twice, racked up $25.00 in late fees, and still haven't been awake for enough of the movie to see Al Pacino shoot anybody.

I was thinking about this the other day when, feeling a bit sentimental, I started watching my family's 1983 Thanksgiving home video.

I was really quite impressed with myself. My film-making has the same effect on me as Francis Ford Coppola's. I've never felt so rested.

VISIONARY
SEEKS 25 OPINIONS

My mother's system for decorating her house was simple:

STEP ONE: Buy furniture that could withstand a nuclear meltdown, and until then, maybe children.

STEP TWO: Saturate everything down to the coffee table with Scotchgard.

STEP THREE: Cover it all in sheets until company came over.

If our home had a theme, I guess it could be described as "Cotton Percale with a primitive art scheme." Not that junk you pay thousands of dollars for in art galleries. But that junk you get for free. Stick figure drawings, and finger paintings, and water colors, and mixed media pieces made out of egg cartons and paper clips and leftover fabric. Basically anything that her three genius daughters created from age one on up was framed and hung on the wall.

This is the house I grew up in. I spent eighteen years living there. And so naturally when I moved into my own home, I completely rejected my mother's overly simplistic style of decorating in favor of my own highly sophisticated, three-step approach:

STEP ONE: I scour the city for every possible paint color, type of fabric, and furniture with no regard for practicality.

STEP TWO: I ask every person I know what he or she thinks, trying to incorporate their twenty-five opinions into what I think my opinion might be.

STEP THREE: I slink back into the showroom, praying that the salesperson who had developed a nervous tic by the time I was done with her last week is on break so I can start the process over with someone new.

Right now I'm preoccupied with determining what color to paint the interior of my home. I know it will be white.

But which white? There are 423 different shades of white. I happen to know this because right now I have one-inch paint samples of each taped to the wall in my living room.

To complicate matters, I'm also thinking of buying a new couch. Of the 57 different couch styles the furniture store featured on its showroom floor, none appealed to me. This explains why I have two tattered black-and-white line drawings from catalogues taped to the wall along with the 423 paint samples. Not to mention 27 three-inch swatches of off-white upholstery fabric.

And, in the saleswoman's own words, "What's a couch without throw pillows?" Add 15 different throw pillow fabric samples ranging from a solid burgundy moiré, to a Southwestern dhurrhie, to a tapestry print depicting little deer and rabbits, to the list of things taped to my wall.

Now to the rank amateur, this wall of 10,248 possible combinations—out of which one must be chosen—might be intimidating. But not to me. Brimming with self-confidence, the creative juices flowing, I stood before the wall ready to make my own decorating statement.

Three minutes later I began inviting girlfriends over.

GIRLFRIEND ONE: I think the combination of "Adobe White" paint with the "Charleston Sofa" done in the off-white nubby cotton with the burgundy moiré throw pillows would add a sense of sophistication to your house. Don't you think?

ME: Yes, maybe you're right.

GIRLFRIEND TWO: If you painted the walls "Palomino White" and then did the "Californian" couch in the dual-tone off-white cotton stripe duck cloth, then threw in the Southwestern pillows for color, your living room would be so casual and inviting. Don't you think?

ME: Yes, maybe you're right.

GIRLFRIEND THREE: I don't think any of these whites is right. I'd like to see a custom color, maybe something in between "Misty White" and "Dove White." Then maybe I'd take the basic frame from the "Charleston" and the pillows from the "Californian" for a more eclectic look. Upholstered in off-white chenille and contrasted with the tapestry throw pillows, it would be arty, soft, and sensual. Don't you think?

ME: Yes, maybe you're right.

Three different women. Three completely different opinions. Perhaps it was time to consider the male perspective:

ME: Well, what do you think?

HIM: Everything looks exactly the same.

ME: Oh, c'mon. Some combination must jump out at you.

HIM: Okay, I like that paint chip.

ME: "Simply White." Hmmm. Interesting. Why "Simply White" instead of "Snow White?"

HIM: I guess I like the name better.

ME: Pretend the paint chips don't have names. Then what would you think?

HIM: I'd think they all look exactly the same.

ME: Well what about the couch?

HIM: (POINTING TO THE "CHARLESTON") That one.

ME: Why?

HIM: (TAPPING HIS FOOT IMPATIENTLY) The game's starting in three minutes.

ME: What about the couch fabric?

HIM: (POINTING TO AN OFF-WHITE ON OFF-WHITE FLORAL) That one.

ME: Why?

HIM: (INCHING HIS WAY OUT OF THE ROOM) I have two and a half minutes left to make a sandwich.

ME: But what about the throw pillows?

HIM: (YELLING FROM THE KITCHEN) Why don't you just shut your eyes?

ME: Good idea. Just shut my eyes and visualize the whole room pulled together.

HIM: No. Shut your eyes and point to one.

I stood there alone contemplating the wall of 10,248 possible combinations. Maybe I should just shut my eyes and try to visualize the whole room pulled together. Maybe then I'd see a room which, after all, would be a reflection of me.

I shut my eyes and saw the room awash in "Barely

White" with the "Californian" couch upholstered in the nubby white cotton fabric, and tapestry throw pillows with little deer and rabbits on them.

Then I saw my dog leaping on top of it with his muddy paws.

Then I saw him attacking the pillows and leaving a trail of deer and rabbit parts strewn all over the house for me to find when I got home from work.

Then I saw a blur of Scotchgard and sheets all over everything until company comes over.

Then I saw myself standing there in sensible shoes and a home perm just like my mother, holding a tray of little hot dogs stuffed with cheese.

Then I ripped all the samples off the wall, marched back into the showroom, and headed directly for the woman with the twitch in her eye.

"We're starting all over again, and I don't care if your body starts to shake!"

Once again, nothing motivates us like our mothers.

THRESHOLD FOR BEAUTY

It's been said that women are the stronger of the sexes. That deep within our very souls we have resources to help us cope with physical pain. Resources that simply do not exist in men.

I plan to draw on these resources someday when I bear children.

But for now, I try to remember that I have them when I go in for a bikini wax.

There I am, lying half-naked on the table. A complete stranger stands over me pouring steaming hot wax on my inner thigh. Moments later it's yanked away. What was on my thigh is now glued to a piece of wax like a mutant creature out of a Boris Karloff movie.

If only hair removal were limited to a woman's inner thighs, it might not be so bad. After all, the main purpose for a bikini wax, bathing suit season, usually begins and ends in the dressing room.

Unfortunately though, getting rid of unwanted hair is a problem for women that lasts twelve months of the year and extends from our upper lips down to our ankles.

I stand in the shower stall, razor in hand, one leg hoisted up on the wall, in a position the women's Olympic gymnastic team has yet dared to try.

I spray foam on my underarms that disintegrates the hair on them, and unclogs the sink when I'm out of Drāno.

I even once paid $60.00 for a method of hair removal called electrolysis. During this session an electrically charged needle jabs your body over and over again as though you're some sort of human voodoo doll, to rid it of the offending hair. They say this is a permanent solution. Could be, though I'll never know. The woman jabbed me in the leg only once before I grabbed my clothes and fled the building.

My favorite, though, is a whirling coil device that came out a couple of Christmases ago. The commercial showed a model happily gliding the whirling coil along her legs while the voice-over touted its benefit: Because her hair was being pulled from its roots, her legs would be hair-free for at least three weeks.

Finally, a solution that made sense. Modern technology triumphs over hair. I grabbed my car keys and raced to the store to purchase my own whirling coil device.

Funny thing about that commercial. I suppose that because it was only thirty seconds long, they had to edit out some of the more dramatic scenes.

Like the one where the model stops happily gliding and starts shrieking, "Help me! There's a lawn mower on my legs!"

Or the one where she stomps off the set and fires her agent.

Or the one where she takes the whirling coil device and runs it across the client's already balding head.

Once I'd patted my freshly coiled legs dry, I took the blood-spotted towel and limped to the laundry room. Rats. I was out of Clorox. But I knew just what to do. I hobbled upstairs and got a jar of the cream I use for upper lip bleaching.

It took the stains right out. And as soon as I patched the holes it had eaten through the fabric, the towel was good as new.

BARBIE LEARNS
TO COPE

Every year the toy companies march out a whole new set of reality-based toys for kids to love and learn from.

One recent addition: A mommy-to-be doll with a flat stomach the child can snap on a second after she expels the tiny plastic baby from the mommy's snap-off pregnant stomach.

Not to be outdone, another toy company has come out with a baby doll that looks so lifelike, you'd swear it was real. They even gave it a permanent fresh talcum powder scent, one that all real mommies and daddies are able to enjoy for approximately twelve seconds after they change little one's all-too-real diapers.

Yet another reality-based entry hit the shelves a few months ago. It's a little doll that gets a perfect golden brown tan in just ten seconds. Though we've yet to hear about it, I'm sure the mommy companion doll who races out to the beach every twelve minutes to reapply number thirty sun block on her precious baby's skin must be somewhere in development.

Last year a woman made a brave attempt to create a female doll that would help little girls build a healthy self-image for themselves. She had a thicker waist, broader hips, and shorter legs than the reigning queen of dolls, Barbie. And because she had flat feet, she could spend her life free of the calf cramps Barbie must suffer after spending the last thirty-four years with her feet crammed into a pair of pointy high heels.

But will any of these dolls ever become a classic? Will any little girl ever be able to love a mommy-to-be doll or a healthy self-image doll as much as nearly every little girl in America has loved her Barbie doll since 1959? I highly doubt it.

Which brings me to my point. If the toy companies are so intrigued with toys based on reality, why don't they just update the classics? After all, who better than Barbie to clue girls in on what really lies ahead in womanhood?

Mattel could start with "Barbie's Special PMS Kit." It would come with a pad you strap on to Barbie's abdomen to mimic bloat. The child would be challenged and enlightened as she tries frantically to zip Barbie into a pair of pants before Ken shows up for their big date.

And speaking of that big date, they might consider developing "Barbie's Guessing Game Kit." It would come with a closet filled with ninety-seven outfits. It would then be the child's job to decipher exactly what Ken had in mind for the evening when he said he'd be over at seven.

She would soon know when the "Good Time Ken" doll rolled in ten minutes later with beer, pizza, and a remote control glued to his hand, wondering why Barbie's all dressed up in a Bob Mackie gown just to watch the NBA finals.

The potential for the reality-based Barbie doll is endless. A "Coping with Financial Ruin Kit," in which a mean little bald man with horn-rimmed glasses from the IRS sits impatiently as Barbie rips through her house in search of her tax records, could provide hours of educational fun.

They could even introduce a one-time-only disposable "Barbie Learns About Human Emotions Kit," in which she causes such a scene at the return counter in the department store that she's too embarrassed ever to go back again.

I was about to mention this concept to a girlfriend the other day but never quite got around to it. We were too busy helping her seven-year-old daughter get Barbie ready for her prom date with Ken.

Minutes before he was to arrive, Kool-Aid was spilled on Barbie's formal, the dog ran off with her corsage, and her right silk slipper was missing—not to be found until the next day when the plumber retrieved what was left of it from the garbage disposal.

Maybe the toy companies and I should reconsider this reality thing. I don't know about little girls. But speaking for Barbie, I think she's got enough to deal with.

A MAN. A WOMAN.
AND THEIR DIRT.

I t is 8:00 A.M. the day his parents and my parents are coming over for dinner. I bound out of bed in high gear, wondering which project to tackle first. There are fresh flowers to be cut and arranged into a centerpiece, hors d'oeuvres to be made, and an appetizer, salad, main course, and dessert to be prepared. The linens need to be washed and ironed and the table needs to be set. Not to mention the house, which is more of a mess than I am right now.

I race outside in my pajamas and wildly begin cutting flowers. I run back inside and fling basil, olive oil, pine nuts, and garlic into the blender. I grab a head of lettuce, rinsing and shredding like a human Veg-o-Matic. I beat the chicken breasts into submission with an iron skillet. I charge to the basement with a bottle of Clorox and the soiled tablecloth in my arms.

An hour and a half later when I'm standing over the kitchen sink ruing the moment I decided to buy the unshelled shrimp because they were cheaper, he wanders out of the bedroom.

"Can I help you do anything?"

"Yes! Yes! Tidy up the house!"

He looks around the dining room and living room beyond. Must be thinking what I'm thinking. The place is a disaster. Dust everywhere. Mail and magazines strewn all over. Grime on the windows. And a floor that's covered with more dog hair than our dog.

Well, thank God it's one thing I don't have to worry about. I dump the shelled shrimp into a bowl and begin a frantic search through my kitchen for a zester. Ladles. Melon ballers. Strainers. A garlic press. Twelve different types of knives. Two melted spatulas. Eight different spoons and a pair of tongs. But no zester. I must have a zester. Why do I not own a zester?!

Three unsuccessful tries with a paring knife, a cut finger, and four mangled limes later, I'm off in search of a store that carries a zester at 9:45 on a Sunday morning.

I grab my purse and am sprinting toward the door when, through the blur, I think I see someone sitting on the couch reading the paper. I stop in my tracks.

"Shouldn't you get started?" I choke out with the last bit of pleasantness left in my voice.

He glances up from the sports section. "I'm done."

"Done?" My eyes dart around the room for signs of the miracle he's allegedly performed in eleven minutes flat. The mail and magazines that were strewn on the floor are now in two piles on the coffee table. But beyond that everything looks exactly the same. "Done. As in *finished*?"

"You said to tidy up. I tidied up."

"But there's dust everywhere."

"Where?"

"There." I point to the coffee table.

"Where?"

"There!" I grab a bottle of Windex and wipe the tabletop clean.

"I don't see any dust."

"Well, of course you don't see any dust because now there isn't any dust. I just wiped it all off."

"Sorry. I guess I didn't notice it."

Didn't notice it? Didn't see it? As if the dust that is the only coordinating theme throughout our house isn't even there?!

"What about the floor?"

"What about it?"

"Do you suppose a wet mop might do it some good?"

He rolls his eyes at me. "Even I know you don't mop carpeting."

"We have wood floors. That's dog hair."

"Oh. Uh, sorry. Guess I didn't see it."

I'm about to suggest that perhaps we need to schedule an eye examination for him when my eyes fixate on the couch.

"You didn't even fluff the pillows."

"The what?"

"The pillows! They're not fluffed! It completely changes the look of the couch when the pillows are big and fluffy!" I go around to each, tossing and punching to illustrate my point. "See?"

He gives me one of those looks I'm sure I'll receive many more of from the nursing staff fifty years from now when I'm in a home somewhere and carrying on a tirade about the gross inadequacies of supermarkets that don't carry zesters. "You know, you're really obsessive."

Me, obsessive? *Me,* obsessive?! I stomp out of the room and slam the door behind me, incredulous that the man who has just accused me of being obsessive is the same man who cleans and polishes his clubs before every golf game as though he's heading into five hours of brain surgery with them.

This is the same man who runs his golf balls through a special scrubbing machine, convinced that even one speck of dirt will completely alter their airborne route to the green.

This is the same man who recently was observed scraping the spikes of his golf shoes with dental floss.

How, then, does the sorry condition of our house completely elude him?

I turn around to polish the door handle I just

smudged when I hear a familiar humming sound coming from the next room.

I open the door and poke my head in to witness a most wonderful sight. Do my eyes deceive me? Has he really just turned on the vacuum cleaner?

Yes! Yes! It has happened. He has seen the error of his ways. He has silently admitted with the flip of a switch that he, too, wants our parents to believe we live in an immaculate home.

I pause in the doorway, taking in the unmatched splendor of a man and a Hoover about to perform a pas de deux through the living room and den.

It's three and a half hours before our guests arrive. There is still time to work a miracle. The house can still be transformed. And I can still find a zester. It can all still happen.

I glance back for one more exhilarating peek. Hmmm.

Well, if I don't have time to create a centerpiece before they get here, I am no longer worried. We can always just clear a place in the middle of the table for his gleaming golf bag, from which I see he's sucking particles of dust with the hose attachment.

RIGHT BODY.
WRONG CENTURY.

I n the sixties, Twiggy had the ideal body type all the women's magazines held up for us to emulate. She had no chest, no waist, no hips, and legs that were like strands of spaghetti. It was the only time in my life I've been able to open a magazine and feel I met all the criteria for the perfect female figure. Possibly because I was ten at the time.

The rules all changed in the seventies when Ali MacGraw made the cover of every major women's magazine. She had breasts. She had a waist. She had hips. And we were supposed to, too.

Then the eighties hit and the pictures we snipped out of magazines and stuck to our refrigerators were of models who looked like they could bench-press three-fifty on a bad day. Muscles were in. So were big breasts. So were narrow hips. The ideal female body type had been completely redefined. And it looked like Arnold Schwarzenegger with a D cup.

Now in the nineties, the magazines have presented us with a whole new, more voluptuous look. Hips are back, so long as they spend half an hour being molded on the StairMaster every day. The waist, while small, needn't feel like a slab of cement to the touch. And the breasts, judging from our most popular models, appear to be getting bigger by the minute.

But most of us have a hard enough time just coping with the basic fear of being fat to worry, from decade to decade, whether or not we're the right version of thin. So most of us are never really free to focus on the one hundred and ninety-seven potential problem areas magazines devote endless time and space trying to help us solve.

Instead, most of us wander from year to year with our bodies divided into three problem areas—top, middle, and bottom—and struggle to make the combination of them not resemble a watermelon.

In the meantime, the male body drifts from generation to generation without ever getting an overhaul. There are no male versions of Twiggy or Cheryl Tiegs or Paulina or Elle MacPherson. No magazine articles in *Esquire* or *GQ* report how big each body part should be in proportion to the others.

Frankly, the only time men are given anything to compare themselves to is when *People* magazine publishes the yearly "Sexiest Man Alive" cover, which not too long ago featured a bald man old enough to date one of the Golden Girls.

Ten years from now, women will be presented with a whole new list of specifications for a perfect figure. Various body parts will get smaller or bigger, rounder or flatter. Hopefully, the breast situation will have stabilized.

In the twenty-first century, I'd prefer to take the time I'd waste poring over magazines identifying my newest problem areas and spend it instead in a museum studying art.

More specifically, I'd devote myself to the work of the Renaissance painters, a brilliant group of men who lovingly highlighted and shadowed every roll of fat on their female subjects.

I will stand there and wonder what it was like to live in a time when there was such a thing as a "perfect size twenty-two."

AUTOMATED
TANTRUMS

For the last week I've been trying to reach my health insurance company over one of those silly little $700.00 claim discrepancies you tend to want to clarify. No cause for alarm though. I'm sure as soon as I speak with a friendly representative there, I'll be able to clear this whole matter up.

I call the 1-800 number on my insurance card and wait for a friendly representative to pick up. Instead, a prerecorded female voice that could double for Nurse Ratched's answers my call:

"Hello. You have reached the Very Limited Coverage Health Care Network. Please note that your call will be taped and monitored. This will give us a leg to stand on if at some point in the future you find some two-bit attorney who wants to sue us."

She continues calmly, never changing the tone of her voice. "If you are using a Touch-tone phone, press one. If you are using a rotary dial phone, we suggest you put the heart attack you are currently having and/or any other medical emergencies on hold until you've purchased a phone that is compatible with our system."

I press one and wait for the friendly insurance representative to pick up the phone. Instead, Nurse Ratched answers again. "Hello. You have now entered the Very Limited Health Care Network inquiry system." She rattles off a series of possible reasons I might have for calling, with corresponding numbers to press for each.

I press one for claim information. I wait for the friendly insurance representative to pick up the phone. No such luck. It's her again grilling me for more information. "Please enter your ID number." "Are you the insured, the insured's spouse, or a corporate benefits manager?" "Is this regarding group benefits or an individual claim?"

With each question I dutifully punch the appropriate button, hoping to finally be connected to a live person. But with every button I push, she's back with a whole new layer of scrutiny:

"When was your office visit? What did you eat that day? What type of underwear are you wearing? For waist-highs, press one. For hip-huggers, press two. For bikinis, press three. For thongs, press four to be connected directly with your mother."

Eight minutes later, just when I believe I'm on the brink of being connected to a live person, my hand slips, accidentally hitting the wrong button. Nurse Ratched doesn't like people who make mistakes. Nurse Ratched disconnects me.

I'm seething. I wonder if a tape of me shrieking at a computerized voice is now being tucked away under a special "disturbed persons" file. I wonder if I should call some two-bit attorney and see if any large sums of money have ever been awarded for emotional distress incurred while using automated phone systems.

Then I begin to marvel at the brilliance of a phone system that lets you avoid all contact with those to whom you'd rather not speak. In fact, I'd like to set one up in my own home. It would field all annoying calls by pre-empting them with a prerecorded series of questions from me doing my best Nurse Ratched voice:

"Hello. You have reached the Guisewite household. If you are interested in selling Ms. Guisewite a service or product, please press the number one now."

"Thank you. Ms. Guisewite cannot be bothered with your lame sales pitch at this time. FYI, she does not need to have her windows washed, her carpet cleaned, or her driveway asphalted. Her yard needs no aeration, fertilization, mowing, pesticides, or pre-emergents, as her dog has spent the last three years systematically destroying it beyond all hope. Her gutters are fine. Though leaking, her roof already has enough tar on it to fill up the La Brea Tar Pits. She's been talked into changing long distance services so many times, she cannot remember the one she's currently using. And she has not, or would not at any time in the future, consider aluminum siding. Ms. Guisewite barely has time to read a paper, let alone a fifteen-volume set of the *Encyclopaedia Britannica,* and her drapes would disintegrate if they were professionally cleaned. Please hang up and do not try again.

"If you are calling seeking a donation for charity, please press the number that corresponds with your cause— I'm calling you today on behalf of Save the 1) Animals, 2) Birds, 3) Fish, 4) Invertebrates, 5) People, 6) Planet, 7) Other. Please keep in mind that Ms. Guisewite is generally a complete sucker for anything that breathes, and will probably blindly write a check to you even though she's never heard of your particular organization. So skip the big speech and go right to the part where you ask her for cash."

Finally, there would be a very special message for my insurance company if they ever get around to calling me back:

"Thank you for calling the Guisewite household. Please note that your call is being taped and monitored. If you are calling regarding the discrepancy in Ms. Guisewite's claim, please begin aimlessly pressing numbers for the next ten minutes, at which point she'll consider throwing out her monitored tape of you trying to use her phone system, if you agree to trash the psychotic tape you have of her trying to use your phone system."

Ultimately, though, I know this tack will bring me

only short-term satisfaction. So I've decided to go about resolving this matter the old-fashioned way. I will write an irate letter to my insurance company and will sit primed at my mailbox waiting for a response from a human being.

I only hope they don't have Nurse Ratched writing letters now, too.

CHEW EACH BITE AT LEAST ONCE

They say that in the nineties corporate America is becoming leaner and meaner. I don't know about the leaner part. But you do tend to get a bit testy when you never have time for a decent lunch.

I was thinking about this the other day while talking to a friend at work with whom I've been trying to make a lunch date for the last month.

"How's Monday for you?" I asked.

"Bad. I have a client meeting at eleven, a client meeting at one, and an appointment with my therapist at two. Maybe Wednesday?"

"Can't make it," I said. "I have to pay all my bills, change the oil in my car before it explodes, clean my house, and pick up groceries for a dinner party I'm having at seven. How about Friday?"

"Friday's no good. My mom's birthday's on Saturday. I have to shop for, wrap, and Federal Express her birthday gift during lunch, plus get my teeth cleaned. Tuesday the tenth good for you?"

"Yes. Perfect," I replied. "So long as we're back in the office by 12:45."

"Good. We'll go to one of those places where the waitress puts a timer down on your table. You know, fifteen minutes or it's free."

"Might take too long. How about McDonald's?"

"Great. Do you mind if we do the drive-through?"

I don't know exactly when it happened. Maybe around the time we learned the Japanese are able to eat, sleep, and take vacations during the twelve minutes a day they aren't beating us at everything else. But somehow, somewhere along the line, the lunch hour has dwindled into the lunch minute.

There are the days when, so consumed with work, I never make it out of my office. It's during these all too frequent moments that I thrill at the sight of things like stray mints in the bottom of my purse, seven-month-old petrified Halloween candy in my pen drawer, and the bag of pork rinds someone gave me last year as a joke.

Then there are the days when I have time to run

only as far as the vending machine for a bite to eat. I run back upstairs hanging on to the shred of hope that once they'd listed the fifty-seven ingredients necessary to make a little package of cheese crackers, they ran out of room to note their considerable nutritional value.

Finally, there are the days I actually make it out of the building, but only to tend to all of the other things I haven't been able to do because I've been so busy working.

Today I was lamenting this problem to a woman I know, who at the moment is enjoying the pleasures of being home with two children, ages three months and two years.

"I haven't sat down and had a decent lunch for a month and a half. Can you believe it?" I said, waiting for her sympathetic reply.

"Lunch . . . Lunch?! Are you joking? It's been a week since I've had time to take a shower, six days since I've had time to slap makeup on my face, and two years and three months since I've been to a restaurant where the main course doesn't come in a Styrofoam box."

I quickly got off the phone, tore open a package of cheese crackers, and spent the next four peaceful minutes alone in my office, savoring each and every bite.

Somehow motherhood gives us all a new perspective.

FLOWERITICUS
DEADUS

Here's a bit of advice for anyone who'd like to enjoy a truly maintenance-free garden:

Go to your nearby gardening center and load up your car with every type of perennial and annual plant you've ever dreamed of growing.

Make sure that each of the plants is accompanied by its little plastic stick that depicts, in color, what the mature flower is supposed to look like. The importance of these photos on the little plastic sticks cannot be stressed enough, as they are crucial to the creation of the maintenance-free garden.

Now pay close attention, because this is where our maintenance-free gardening lesson gets a little tricky. Gently pull the little plastic sticks with the pictures of the flowers on them out of their containers and arrange and rearrange them in your bed until you've created a color palette that is pleasing to the eye.

Congratulations. Your garden is planted. You may now feel free to discard the planting materials that came along with your little plastic sticks.

Yes, it may sound radical, but had you actually made the mistake of planting the real thing, you would have been glued to a gardening regimen that starts May 31, when you turn on your garden hose and begin watering the flowers, and ends September 30, when you turn off the hose and attempt to pry your hand from it.

The lovely pictures on the little plastic sticks will not turn brown if you forget to water them. In fact, they'll keep their brilliant colors all summer long while you're off doing all the fun summer activities that people who do not have gardens are able to enjoy—like taking vacations, swimming, eating, and sleeping.

Also, to my knowledge, bugs are not attracted to pictures of flowers on little plastic sticks. They are only interested in the real thing. In fact, just murmur under your breath that you're thinking of planting a garden and bugs will come parading in from every corner of the earth to mow down everything in your yard except the grass, which desperately needs cutting.

At first you'll obsess over figuring out ways to get rid of these creatures. Later you'll obsess over figuring out at exactly what point in your life you became one of those people who's able to carry on an hour-long conversation with your neighbor over garden slug control.

Like bugs, dogs have a remarkable predilection for staking out a good garden. Just drive down any street and know that wherever you see a dog weighing seventy pounds or more sprawled out in the afternoon sun, there's a prize-winning perennial bed nearby. Most likely, it's right underneath him.

I can't speak for other dogs, but I believe my dog engages in this particular activity because he wants to protect what he thinks is truly important to me. Robbers could clean me out of house and home. But I know my trusty dog would bravely lie there heading off any attempts by thieves to make off with my begonias.

The other nice thing about the little plastic sticks with the pictures of flowers on them is that, unlike real flowers, they will never grow. Instead, they'll remain neatly arranged in exactly the order you spent three months charting and plotting out for them.

Hostas will not stampede over Primrose. Day Lilies will not trample Cosmos. And what you thought would be a lovely border plant will not grow to reach the height of your roof.

And because the pictures on the little plastic sticks are so vivid, you will readily be able to discern all intruders. You will not, for example, spend an entire summer nurturing, fertilizing, and watering a species, only to have a friend point out to you that it's a weed with roots so ominous that it's probably just as well you leave it alone because if you attempt to yank it out, your house will come out of the ground right along with it.

Finally, there's the healthy glow that can be achieved only by staying out of your yard. You will never again be in the middle of a presentation only to realize that your clients are transfixed not by the charts you're holding up, but by your hands, which are embedded with dirt and have calluses on them the size of half-dollars. You will never again need to search the city for a pair of patterned pantyhose that matches the rash you have on your legs.

Instead, you'll be able to relax and enjoy your garden, which, after all, is supposed to be what gardening is all about.

You will don the Smith and Hawken gardening outfit you spent $80.00 on before you realized that the models in the catalogue in their crisply pressed uniforms were approximately three miles from the nearest piece of dirt. And you will drift off in your Adirondack chair pondering life, nature, and what kind of AstroTurf to use to cover up your dead grass.

THE GREAT DEPRESSION OF '85

GLOBAL CORRECTNESS

OLD WAY

NEW WAY

PAPER BAG FROM 1942, STILL BEING USED

$22 CANVAS ECO-SAC, WASHED WEEKLY IN $15 A BOX SUDS-FREE SOAP

I stood outside showing my mother the $25.00 worth of compost I had just hauled home from the garden center:

"See, Mom, it's all natural, so my garden can thrive completely chemical-free."

"Why in the world would you buy compost when

you can make it yourself with leftovers and grass clippings without spending a penny?"

Slightly annoyed, I took her into the kitchen to show her the $30.00 recycling bin I'd just bought:

"See, Mom, it's separated into three compartments, one for tin, one for glass, and one for plastic."

"The whole bin's made of plastic. Why don't you just use paper bags?"

"I use paper bags to store plastic bags so I can return them to the grocery store for recycling."

"If you reused the same plastic bags over and over, you'd never have to return them."

I hastily tucked away the $22.00 "Eco-Sac" order form I was about to show her, realizing that, after all, a woman who's rinsed and reused her original box of Baggies she bought in 1971 can't really be lectured on the value of recycling.

A woman who used only cloth diapers, then turned them into cleaning rags, then used the remaining shreds for doll stuffing, can hardly be to blame for turning our nation's landfills into one giant diaper bin.

A woman who considers a pair of pantyhose that are shredded down to the ankles perfectly wearable because "if you're wearing pants, who'll ever know?" can never be accused of being wasteful.

I grew up thinking she was a complete fanatic, not to mention a person with incredibly unattractive hosiery.

"You don't know what it was like to live through the Depression," she would say as I rolled my eyes while watching her spend an eternity unwrapping a gift with the precision of a brain surgeon, so she could wrap another gift with the paper later.

THE GREAT DEPRESSION OF '85

"You don't know what it was like to live through the Depression," she would say, cutting me off midway through one of my fifteen-second long "mu-thrrrrrr's," as I witnessed her rinsing tuna casserole off yesterday's piece of aluminum foil so she could use it to wrap that night's precious leftover chicken wing.

"You don't know what it was like to live through the Depression," she would say each time I let out an exasperated sigh as she mixed together vinegar and water to clean the floors, instead of buying one of the seven hundred ready-made cleansers from the supermarket.

But my mother was wrong. I do know what it was like to live through the Depression.

It began on Earth Day in 1985 when I sat her down at the kitchen table and showed her the $35.00 environmental awareness game I was about to order for my niece.

"See, Mom, it teaches children about the delicate balance of the rain forest's ecosystem."

She whipped out a bag of empty toilet paper tubes she's been saving since 1958 and emptied them on the table.

"With a few crayons, paste, scissors, and a little imagination, she could make her own rain forest out of these."

My depression deepened when I dragged her to the specialty store at the mall that carries only 100% natural, cruelty-free cosmetics and skin-care products.

"See, Mom, when you buy from a store like this, you can be sure no animals have suffered. Take this beauty mask here. It's made of avocado and olive oil."

"Hmm. Just like this one," she said, pulling from

her purse the baby jar filled with the slimy green concoction she's been making and slapping on her face for the last twenty years.

My depression peaked when I escorted her into the women's department and showed her the environmentally correct jeans I wanted to buy.

"See, Mom, these jeans are labeled 'unbleached' so we know that when we buy them we're joining the fight to keep our water clean."

"Why would you buy bleached jeans in the first place? They make you look like a bum," she said. Then she looked approvingly down at what she was wearing, which used to be a pair of white cotton pants. But then she took all the seams out, added panels in the front and back, and shortened it. So now it's a white cotton skirt.

Could it be? Could my mother with her homemade compost and old paper bags and old pantyhose and old aluminum foil and old Baggies and old empty toilet paper tubes and remade clothing have completely out-recycled me?

Like any self-respecting person who's racked up $500.00 on her Visa card saving the planet, I was not about to give up.

Surely the day would come when my mother would see that my generation's environmental conscientiousness was superior to her own.

As luck would have it, the very next day I arrived at work to find that my company was starting a recycling program.

I could barely wait to call my mother and gloat, knowing that she would be impressed by the sheer size of this operation.

Styrofoam cups were banished from the building, and all five hundred of us received plastic recycling bins accompanied by a two-page memo categorizing every type of paper and noting its acceptance or nonacceptance in the program. (IN: "White and colored letterheads, note paper, typing paper, legal paper, NCR paper, adding machine tapes, pamphlets, brochures, uncoated copy paper, call slips." OUT: "Carbon paper, forms with carbon intertwined, chipboard [such as backs of legal pads], coated copy paper, sheets covered by adhesive.")

Huh?

And those were just the instructions under heading number one: OFFICE PAPER.

About a week later when I had waded my way down to heading number seven, FILE FOLDERS, and was trying to decipher whether or not the fluorescent orange one that I was holding in my hand counted as an IN ("manila, white, tan, or light colors"), or as an OUT ("deep tones, red rope, brown or draft, Pendaflex, or string- or cloth-backed"), my secretary dropped off another memo.

Fortunately, this one was much easier to understand: "To all employees. Re: Recycling Program. Please do not throw food and Styrofoam cups into recycling bins."

Yes, a few fellow employees, who apparently had made even less of memo number one than I had, had been tossing their half-eaten bologna sandwiches and bootleg Styrofoam cups into the bins.

I sat there with both memos in front of me able to think of nothing but what my mother would say: "Styrofoam cups? Why on earth would you waste money on

Styrofoam cups when you can rinse out a mug or a glass for free?" Or, "Why do you waste so much paper anyhow? You know if you wrote on both sides you could cut down on your paper use by half." Or, "Someone's throwing away a half-eaten lunch? Don't they know there are people starving in—"

Yeah, Mom, maybe some of your ideas aren't so bad after all.

But still, the next time I hit the mall for a new $15.00 tube of cruelty-free lipstick, I'm stopping at the department store and getting you some new pantyhose.

A FRENZY OF
RELAXATION

S top. Wait. Hold everything. I spent three months planning this vacation, six days trying to unwind on it, and now on day seven I'm standing in the waiting area clutching the plane ticket that will bring me home.

"We will now begin boarding flight 405 nonstop service to Detroit. Will those passengers seated in first class and those passengers needing assistance please board the plane now."

No. We can't be boarding yet. I have a suitcase stuffed with five hundred dollars' worth of clothing, half of which never even made it out of my bag.

I searched the city in the dead of winter for this summer wardrobe. There's the peach sundress with matching shoes, purse, sun hat, and a strand of multicolored beads that if you're standing one inch away from me in broad daylight you'll notice includes a reoccurring peach bead that ties the whole outfit together.

There's the skin-tight black linen cocktail dress that will fit perfectly as soon as I lose ten pounds, which if I could just stay here for twenty-four more hours, I'm sure I would.

There are coordinated shorts and tops, shoes and socks, accessories and headbands. Not to mention the two-piece bathing suit that so far I've only had the nerve to wear in my hotel room, in the bathroom, with the door bolted shut.

Fifteen minutes until I have to be on the plane. If I start now I could hurl myself in and out of the ladies' room seven times and wear each of these outfits for one minute each. I think I'll start with the peach one. Maybe the lady at the ticket counter will notice the matching bead thing . . .

"Flight 405 service to Detroit now boarding rows fifteen through thirty. Please have your tickets ready."

No. It's too late for changing outfits. What I really need to do is spend the next eight minutes relaxing. That's what the whole purpose of a vacation is supposed to be, right? You spend fifty-one weeks out of the year building up to a nervous breakdown, and one week letting it all go so that you can go home and start the whole process over again.

But it's not all gone. It took me four days of this trip before I stopped bolting out of bed at 6:00 A.M. worrying I was going to be late for a meeting. And three days to be able to leave my hotel room without thinking I'd forgotten my briefcase. And only yesterday, my secretary forbade me to call the office anymore:

"Yes, everything's fine. No, nothing's going on. Relax, for heaven's sake. You're on your vacation!"

She's right. I am on my vacation, so that means I should relax. So relax is what I will do. I pull out two of the three-hundred-page novels I had meant to read on my vacation to see if there is one I can possibly skim through in the next seven minutes.

Better yet, I could use this seven minutes of relaxation time more wisely by studying one of my foreign language tapes. I stick in the cassette and push the play button on my Walkman:

"*Bonjour.* This means "hello" in French . . ."

"Flight 405 is now boarding rows nine through fourteen."

That's me. I'm in fourteen C. There's no time to learn French. I have postcards to write. Meaningful gifts to buy. I grab my things and race to the airport gift shop. Not that I couldn't have bought beautiful trinkets for all of my friends and family three days ago when I was standing in the middle of a bazaar loaded with fabulous handwoven baskets, all for under $5.00. Maybe I'll find something better, I thought. I now stand at the cash register paying six times that for cheap souvenir

T-shirts, hoping that no one will notice the airport logos on them.

"Flight 405 now boarding all rows."

No. I will not board this plane yet. I have three minutes of vacation left and Delta Air Lines is not going to rob me of them. I stare out the terminal window and take in all the breathtaking beauty there is to be taken in when the view is of a row of DC-10's.

I decide that I will spend this final two and a half minutes reflecting on the last thirty-two years of my life and setting realistic goals for my future.

But suddenly all I'm able to think about is how much I miss my dog. I stand there wondering if he misses me, too. I wonder if he thinks I abandoned him. Will he leap up and get his muddy paws all over my brand-new transitional tropics-to-subzero travel outfit for which I scoured the city? Or will he ignore me as punishment for not spending my week's vacation playing in the park with him?

No matter how cold it is when I get home, I promise myself I will take him for the walk of his life. We'll come back in and he'll lie beside me and I'll pet him as I grab a cup of coffee and start sorting through the bills.

Oh God. Did I pay the electric bill? Or did I write the check and plan on mailing it at the airport the day I left? I dig through my purse and find it all wadded up on the bottom, gooped up with number thirty, fifteen, and eight sun block.

And the coffee maker. Did I really turn it off? I know I checked it three times before I left, but I was in such a hurry. Maybe I only thought it was off. I called and asked my neighbor to check on it for me, and she said she would. But what if knowing what an obsessive worrier I am, she assumed I'd checked on it three times and didn't do the all-important quadruple check for me?

"Flight 405 is now ready for departure. All passengers should be on board."

Get me out of here! I want to go home! I want my dog! I want my own cozy bed! I want all my overdue bills! I want my freezing house with no electricity!

I glance over at the lady standing next to me. She too has four carry-on bags and a purse that should've been checked through as luggage. We stare at each other for a moment and then both of us bolt for the plane to scramble for the one remaining overhead compartment.

Only fifty-one more weeks until I get to do this all over again.

SHOP 'TIL YOU'RE NO LONGER SPEAKING

've never known a man who had the stamina required to shop with a woman.

I think this is because men's shopping needs are so entirely different from our own. A man's life in the fashion world goes something like this:

AGE ONE DAY THROUGH TWO YEARS: Diapers and a shirt.
AGE TWO YEARS THROUGH REST OF LIFE: Pants and a shirt.

So long as they can find twelve spare minutes every few years to locate an assortment of these two items, most men can get by.

Unlike women, who need six months just to adjust to whatever the fashion designers are hurling at us this year, three months to find it in our size, and three more months to locate the shoes, purses, hosiery, and accessories necessary to complete the look. It all works out so that by the time we exit the last store, we have approximately the length of the mall parking lot before what we're wearing is out of style and it's time to turn around and start the whole shopping process over again.

If nothing else, this basic difference has been responsible for some of the more forgettable moments I've shared with men.

I appear from the fitting room to get his opinion on a navy blazer:

"Well, what do you think?"

"It looks great. Buy it."

"I can't buy it. It's the first one I tried on."

"Well, how many do you have to try on before you decide?"

"There are twenty-three women's stores in the mall, three jacket styles I'm interested in, and four shades of navy I like. That makes two hundred seventy-six possible navy jackets. Unless, of course, I decide to go with the camel color."

He makes a clucking sound with his tongue I've never heard before. Moments later he bolts for the electronics department.

On another day I stand at the makeup counter with seventeen different shades of mauve lipstick on the back of my hand:

"Which one looks better on me?"

"How can I tell? None of them are on your lips."

"I can't put them on my lips. If I put them on my lips, they'll all smear together into one color."

"Okay. That one," he says, pointing.

"That one?" But which one is "that one"? I begin frantically reapplying all seventeen shades of mauve lipstick on the inside of my arm, trying to determine which one is "that one," when I hear a familiar clucking sound and look up to see him escaping to the sporting goods department.

In yet another episode, I'm seated in the shoe department, surrounded by six pairs of black suede shoes, with one pair on my feet:

"How do you like them?"

"You already have twelve pairs of black shoes at home."

"Yes, but these have little tassels on the front and a low heel. They're completely different."

"Fine. I like them."

"Better than this pair without the tassel and the slightly higher heel?" I ask, bending over and picking up the new contenders.

Funny. Not even a cluck this time to cue his exit.

It's experiences like these that have eliminated men and established women as my premier shopping companions. Specifically, I love to shop with my mother, a woman whose capacity to shop equals my own, and who is limited only by store hours and an occasional stop in the restroom.

She and I once conducted a seven-hour, three-mall search for a pair of earrings that would pick up the muted greenish-gray flecks in a tweed jacket we'd found.

Another time when we were shopping together, my mom asked the sales clerk if we could take four blouses outside to check their color in natural light. Not an unreasonable request when you consider that once we got them outside, all were the wrong shade of white.

Yet another time my mother called me from a pay phone halfway across the world not to tell me of the wonders of Notre Dame and the Louvre, but to make sure I halted my search for a short-waisted navy sweater because she'd just found one for half price on one of their bus tour stops.

Is it trivial pursuit? A predisposition to consume ourselves with subtleties of outer appearance that somehow is missing in men?

Hardly. I prefer to think of the twelve hundred

hours I've spend shopping with my mother as the basis of a unique bond—strengthened in women's sportswear, sealed in hosiery, and of course, cemented indelibly the next day as we stand together at the return counter waiting to start all over again.

SMART WOMEN,
HUMILIATING CHOICES

It occurs to me that there should be a three-day mandatory waiting period after reading *Cosmopolitan* magazine before a woman is allowed to have contact with a member of the opposite sex.

If this were so, if there were three short days during which a woman could consider the probable consequences of heeding this magazine's advice, I'm quite sure that the following humiliating moments would not have taken place:

HUMILIATING MOMENT NUMBER 1

Shortly after reading an article entitled "What Every Man Wants, but Will Never Admit," Jennifer McKenzie* of Minneapolis, Minnesota, goes to a New Year's Eve party with her boyfriend Stewart. At the appropriate moment, she leans over and flirtatiously whispers in his ear, "I'm not wearing any underwear."

To which he says, "What? I can't hear you."

"I'm not wearing any underwear," she whispers a bit more loudly.

"What? What's that?"

"I said I'm not wearing any underwear!" she hisses.

"You're not wearing any what?"

"Underwear!! Underwear!!" she yells at the top of her lungs.

The ballroom falls silent. The deathly quiet is punctuated only by the sound of a pair of heels clicking across the marble floor to the nearest exit.

HUMILIATING MOMENT NUMBER 2

Shortly after reading an article entitled "How to Make Him Lust After You Twenty-four Hours a Day," Shelly

* All names have been changed to protect the hideously embarrassed.

Barns of Atlanta, Georgia, calls her boyfriend at work. The first words out of her mouth are "I want you Steven."

"Um. Not now," he whispers.

"Yes now, Steven Phillips. I want you this very minute."

"There are seventeen people in my office."

"Oh, um—"

"We're on speaker phone."

"My, what an incredibly small world it is. Wrong number. Wrong Steven Phillips. Pardon the ring—" (CLICK)

HUMILIATING MOMENT NUMBER 3

Shortly after reading an article entitled "Risque Business: Lingerie Styles That Will Set Your Boudoir on Fire," Martha Jones of Buffalo, New York, races to the nearest lingerie department and purchases a black merry widow with red lace trim.

She hurries home, hooks herself into it, and proceeds to fling herself onto her bed, practicing the pose she will strike when her boyfriend Jonathan arrives home from work.

Oh, the look in his eye when he sees me, she thinks, tossing her head back onto the pillow.

Unfortunately, she never gets to see the look in Jonathan's eye.

However, she does get to see the look in her mother's eye after begging her to come free her from the bedspread in which twenty-five merry widow hooks have become hopelessly entangled.

HUMILIATING MOMENT NUMBER 4

Shortly after reading an article entitled "How to Let Him Know What Drives You Wild," Tracy Moore of Dayton, Ohio, composes a saucy love poem to her boyfriend, Jeff, spritzes it with perfume, and drops it in the mailbox.

Four minutes later Jeff calls her and announces that he wants to break up.

Two minutes later, Tracy Moore of Dayton, Ohio, takes a sledgehammer to the mailbox and is arrested for tampering with government property.

HUMILIATING MOMENT NUMBER 5

Shortly after reading an article entitled "Business Woman by Day. Temptress by Night," Phyllis Stockard of Terre Haute, Indiana, shows up at her boyfriend Edward's apartment wearing nothing but a trench coat and a pair of four-inch stiletto heels. When he opens the door, she coyly says, "I've got on a little surprise for you."

"Wait! Wait! I want to see it, too!" his mother says, racing in from the kitchen.

"Your mother's here?"

"I just popped in. Let me take your coat."

"I'll get it! I'll get her coat!" his father says, racing in from the living room.

"Your father's here?!"

"Mom. Dad. Please. I'll get her coat," Edward says, moving toward her.

"No, really. I think I'll leave it on."

"Don't be ridiculous. Give me your coat," he persists, reaching for her shoulder.

"Get back! Get back all of you!!" she shrieks, limping backward on one stiletto heel while wildly waving the other one at them with her right hand. "So help me God, I'm keeping this coat on if it's the last thing I do!!"

Come to think of it, maybe what we need here isn't a three-day waiting period. Maybe what we need is an outright ban.

ONE BIG HAPPY
TIME BOMB

W hile the whole country was arguing about family values, I never heard one person zero in on the real problem. During the hours of the day when we're vivacious, pleasant, and giving, we're stuck with the people at the office. During the hours of the day when we're exhausted, cranky, and ready to strangle someone, we're surrounded by our loved ones.

Case in point: At 7:30 this morning, when the man of my dreams last laid eyes on me, I had stringy wet hair, a piece of toast sticking out of my mouth, and was crawling around on all fours with one eye shut. Our early morning quality time was spent engaged in this conversation:

HIM: We're out of coffee cream!
ME: Don't come near me! You might step on my contact lens!

Three hours later at 10:30 A.M., when I met with an aggravating client, I was a completely different person. Not only was I effusive and articulate, my hair and makeup were perfect, I could see out of both eyes, and my upper lip was no longer sprinkled with toast crumbs.

At 7:30 P.M. the man of my dreams and I were finally reunited after a long day at the office. While we lay sprawled at opposite ends of the couch in silence, his hand flapped limply around for the phone to call in our pizza order. My toe aimlessly poked at the remote control in an attempt to stifle the only person in the room with anything cheerful to say—Mary Hart.

Compare this with the lunch I'd had with my boss seven hours earlier. Each of us coiffed, fluffed, puffed, and Binaca-ed, we spent a lively hour over grilled swordfish discussing everything from the fall of communism to whether or not the man seated at the table next to us was wearing a toupee.

• • •

At 8:30 P.M. my dog begged me to play with him. I flung the ball across the room once before drifting off to sleep by the time he returned with it twenty-four seconds later. This is woman's best friend we're talking about here. A creature whose every waking moment revolves around worshiping me.

If only I could have mustered one fifth of the energy I'd had five hours ago at 3:30, when seventeen co-workers and I Xeroxed our faces on the copy machine and made a birthday card for a woman in accounting I barely even know.

And I'm only going home to one man and a dog. What about all the other people I see around me at the height of evening rush-hour traffic?

I look in my rearview mirror and notice a woman dressed in a power suit with an empty infant seat next to her. I can just imagine that reunion. She's exhausted and stressed and about to pick up a two-year-old who peaked on Oreos at three o'clock.

Next to me I see a woman with two screaming Cub Scouts, a filthy Brownie, a yapping dog, and a morose teenager hanging her head out the back window. The chance of this woman cheerfully putting dinner on the table like June Cleaver is about as likely as her having time for an apricot bubble bath and makeover before her husband gets home from work.

A lane over, I see a man honking and cursing at the person ahead of him to speed up. Will all this anxiety miraculously evaporate by the time he gets home? Or will he still have the steering wheel clenched in his hands when he walks through the front door to greet his family?

In my opinion, family values would improve dramatically if we simply restructured the day so that we would spend the hours between 10:00 A.M. and 3:00 P.M.—when each of us is at our best—with those we care about most. Let the business of the day be conducted from 7:00 to 10:00 A.M. and 3:00 to 8:00 P.M. Let people whose names we probably won't even remember twenty-five years from now deal with us when we have all the charm and goodwill of an IRS auditor.

It's an idea I had at 10:30 one morning while riding high on the crest of a caffeine/doughnut buzz. An idea I couldn't wait to tell the man of my dreams when I saw him next at 7:00 P.M.

Such brilliant conceptual thinking should be rewarded with dinner at a five-star restaurant. Perhaps a complimentary back rub would even be in order.

And I'm sure both the meal and the massage would have been mine, had my remaining shred of enthusiasm not been lost when I tripped over his galoshes on my way into the house. And had he still had the physical stamina to pull the lever on the recliner to the "Up" position.

IN MEMORY OF A
JELLO MOLD

I stood opening cupboard after cupboard, in search of
the jello mold that has been a part of my mother's
kitchen since 1957.

"Where's the jello mold, Mom?" I called to her in
the other room.

"Third cupboard on the right."

"I can't find it."

"Here, sweetie. It's right here," she said, running in and pulling out a jello mold I'd never seen before.

"Not that one. Where's the other one?"

"That old thing? I gave it to Goodwill."

My head was flooded with memories as I stared at her in disbelief. This was no ordinary jello mold. This was **our** jello mold. Our mother/daughter jello mold. The one that she and I had poured bright red jello into together until she read the articles about how Red Dye number 19 is a cancer-causing agent, after which we switched to the infinitely safer bright green. How could she so callously toss it into the Goodwill box right next to the old mixer I couldn't have cared less about, as if they weren't any different?

The same thought crossed my mind a week later when I found out she had given away her mother's set of crimson-colored juice glasses.

"Mother, how could you?" I snapped.

"But you thought they were ugly."

"I still do. But they were Grandma's."

"*She* thought they were ugly."

"I used to sit on her lap and drink cherry Cokes out of them!"

"They were chipped."

"You served milk out of them at my sixth birthday party!"

"They were taking up too much room."

"Too much room?! You mean to tell me you can make room for Aunt Rena's little wooden Christmas sleigh, but you couldn't find twelve inches of extra space for Grandma's crimson glasses?!"

"Oh. Um, Aunt Rena's little wooden Christmas sleigh?" she said, looking down at her feet.

"Oh, no, Mom. You couldn't have. Not Aunt Rena's little wooden Christmas sleigh. Not—"

"But it was falling apart."

"Possibly because your three daughters have spent the last thirty-seven Christmases playing with it!"

"But I'll buy a new one."

"I don't want a new one. I want the old one!" I choked out, spinning around and bolting for the basement to see if anything was left of my past.

"I'll find one to match all the new Christmas ornaments!" she promised, chasing after me.

"You didn't," I said, stopping midway down the stairs.

"Oops."

"Great Grandma's hand-blown partridge ornaments are gone?"

"They were broken!"

"I don't care if all that was left were their beaks, Mother! They've been in our family since 1902!"

I bounded down the rest of the stairs and into her storage room, my mother right at my heels.

"Here, sweetie. This heap on the floor is the 'out' pile. The stuff on the shelves stays."

I grabbed an old blue coat from the top of the heap and clutched it in my arms. "I used to play dress-up in this coat at Grandma's," I said, looking up at her littered shelves. "Why don't you toss out that hideous old popcorn ball wreath instead?"

She looked at me incredulously. "You made that popcorn ball wreath for me in the second grade."

"But what could possibly prompt you to throw out my collection of sand from the Great Lakes and keep that mildewy old hat?"

"But it's not just any mildewy old hat. It's Grandpa's mildewy old hat."

"Then toss that cracked china set!"

"Our mother/daughter tea party set? Absolutely not! Dump the smelly bear!"

"Mr. Tootles? Not on your life!"

We sat there for the next two hours together, telling each other the stories behind our favorite objects, yearning for our pasts, while at the same time both yearning for something much larger. And I think you know it's storage space I'm talking about.

FREE AS A BIRD.
$900.00 IN THE HOLE.

I accepted the fact that if I wanted to be safe, I needed to commit myself to a monogamous relationship. But at least if I ever felt like fleeing, I could always jump on a plane whenever I wanted.

I accepted the fact that if I wanted to be secure, I needed to commit myself to a job. But at least if I ever got fed up, I could always jump on a plane whenever I wanted.

I accepted the fact that if I wanted to live a long and healthy life, I needed to commit myself to a workout program. But at least if I could no longer bear the regimen, I could always jump on a plane whenever I wanted.

All I needed to do was call the airline when the mood struck me and make last-second arrangements to go anywhere, anytime I wanted. I was free as a bird and stuffing myself with complimentary peanuts and beverages all the way there.

Then the airlines went to war and offered cheap fares to anyone willing to make a commitment months in advance.

Then everyone called and ordered their tickets.

Then there weren't any seats left.

Then there was nowhere left for the uncommitted to jump except for maybe into our cars and directly into a traffic jam on the interstate.

And yet knowing all of this I continue to hang on to the dream that I can still somehow jump on a plane whenever I want, and go anywhere I choose. A dream that is shattered for me every year in mid-July when my father calls:

"Hi, honey. Just checking to see if you've booked your Christmas flight."

"Dad, it's July fifteenth. I can jump on a plane whenever I want."

"Well, before you know it, all the good fares will be gone and all the planes will be booked up."

"Dad, don't worry. It's July fifteenth. I'll find a plane to jump on."

The conversation is just as aggravating to my father

as it is to me. After all, for a man who's been committed to the same woman, house, and family for over forty-five years, it's hard to understand why his daughter can't commit to a lousy airline ticket five months in advance. Besides, with him not knowing when I'm coming down, how can he possibly make our holiday dinner reservations? After all, it's already July fifteenth and things do get booked up.

The irony in all of this is that I know I will visit my parents at Christmas. I do it every year. But exactly what day? What time? What airline? I'm determined to hang on to this freedom, miniscule as it may be.

I hang on to it in September when my mother calls:

"Hi, honey. Just wondering when you're planning on coming down for Christmas. Your father and I were out with the Otters last night and their daughter and her family are all booked to come on December twenty-third. Have been for three—"

I click the answering machine off before I learn how long the Otters' daughter, her husband, and kids have had their reservations booked. Three weeks? Three months? Three years? Who knows?

Of course they can't just jump on a plane whenever they want because they have kids. And frankly it's kind of hard to jump anywhere when you have the two hundred extra pounds of apparatus necessary to transport a one- and a three-year-old strapped to your back.

Not me, though. I will be traveling alone and I am determined to jump.

I cling to my freedom in October when I discuss the holidays with a friend of mine whom I'm sure will not give in to the system:

"So what are you and Frank doing for Christmas?"

"We're flying to Honolulu on December eighteenth. Then it's off to Maui on the twenty-third, over to Kauai on the twenty-sixth, back to the mainland on the twenty-ninth, and home in time for New Year's on the thirty-first. You?"

"Oh, I'm just going to jump on a plane and visit my folks."

"When?"

"When? Who knows when? The twenty-third. Maybe the twenty-fourth. You know me, I like to keep things kind of loose."

"Good luck. Frank and I have had our reservations since July."

I peer at her closely, suddenly aware I have a defector in my midst. Is it the prospect of planning something with Frank that's gotten to her? Or the fact that she's traveling somewhere slightly more exotic than my parents' house, that's compelled her to leap to the other side along with my folks, the Otter children, and all their luggage?

She may have her Christmas day luau brunch booked at the Maui Ramada Inn, but I've still got my freedom. I can still jump on a plane whenever I want.

In November I cling not only to my freedom but also to my calendar, which I'm sure will soon be loaded with holiday party invitations. How can I book a flight to my parents' with so much possibility lying ahead? Surely some black tie gala will come up that not only will give me a guideline for planning my trip, but, more important, will justify why I've just spent $200.00 on this year's black velvet holiday party dress.

On December twelfth I cling not to my freedom, but

to the hope that the sales lady won't notice the giant bold-type "NO RETURN ON FORMAL WEAR" stamp on my receipt.

The black tie gala invites must have gotten lost in the mail along with the tree trimming party and casual holiday get-together invitations. And I'm not going to be one of those pathetic people who, as a last resort, wears her holiday formal wear to the office Christmas party all the while trying to keep it free of fruit ambrosia and chip dip stains.

Suddenly I'm desperate to see my family. I'm desperate to be part of the schedule my parents have had planned since July. I'm desperate to be committed to something other than a $200.00 black velvet holiday party dress I know I'll never wear.

I can jump on a plane whenever I want and I want to jump this very second.

I call the airlines to book a reservation:

"Yes, I'd like to jump on a plane to Sarasota on the twenty-second."

"We're booked."

"Can I jump on one the twenty-third?"

"Booked."

"I'll take anything you've got. Just get me there!"

I wind up paying $900.00 for what five months ago would have been a $150.00 airfare.

I wind up having to switch planes three times for what five months ago would have been a direct flight.

And when all is said and done, I wind up having to take a three-hour, seven-stop bus ride to Sarasota from Tampa because all the flights there were already booked.

In retrospect, I would like to think that there are other safer and less costly ways to fulfill my need to be uncommitted in some area of my life.

Like maybe I could try being uncommitted to a specific brand of fiber-enriched cereal for a while. Or maybe throw caution to the winds and not always floss my teeth in the exact same order.

All I know is, it's barely January and I'm already feeling the need to jump.

7,423 KODAK
MOMENTS

My family's photo organization problem began forty-seven years ago, the day my parents were married and never got around to putting a wedding album together. It has gotten increasingly worse with every roll of film taken every year since.

It's an organizational nightmare that started out in black and white, moved through a brief stint on Polaroid, and then on to color. It transcends every speed of film we've ever used and every type of camera we've ever owned.

By now every member of my family has only the most up-to-date photographic equipment. Though none of us has the state-of-the-art piece of gadgetry that we all really need: the little device that will take the pictures out of the packages and place them into the albums for us.

Until that day, we're all left to our own methods of organization. My mother prefers the stuffing-the-packages-of-pictures-into-the-grocery-bags technique. My sister favors the cramming-them-into-the-drawer method. I myself prefer the jamming-them-into-the-cardboardboxes system.

It wouldn't be so bad if we were the type of family able to limit our photo taking to one token snapshot per family gathering.

But we're not. We live for these spontaneous family photo opportunities:

"Is it time to open our presents yet?" my niece asks at 7:10 A.M. Christmas Day.

"Not yet. Aunt Mickey's looking for her mascara."

"Can we open them now?" she begs at 7:30 A.M.

"Just as soon as your Aunt Cathy puts on her blush and your mommy takes out her hot rollers."

"Now?" she pleads at 7:55 A.M.

"Grandma just needs to finish pressing her silk pajamas."

Finally, at 8:00 A.M., the gift-opening frenzy begins, and so does the picture taking. The recipient, gift, and gift-giver are shot together, separately, and in different formations during all points of the gift-opening process —every spontaneous moment shot and reshot until we get it right: "No. Look as surprised as you did eight shots ago when you first opened the *Little Mermaid* doll but Aunt Mickey was on the wrong shutter speed. That's it. Now let me reload and we'll get the whole thing over in arty black and white . . ."

We relish the challenge of finding a one-hour photo lab that's open on Christmas Day.

And then two hours later, after we've sorted through all of them and picked the eighty-five "keepers" we each have to have copies of, we load up our cameras and begin feverishly snapping away again.

There are pictures of us eating Christmas breakfast, pictures of us eating Christmas lunch, pictures of us eating Christmas dinner, and pictures of us in our Christmas food comas at 10:00 P.M. as we try to stay awake to watch the video footage of it all.

Weeks later we're all in our individual homes with package after package of the copies we've exchanged. It is now time to make a clearheaded attempt to pull the winners from the losers and organize them into our stacks of empty photo albums.

But it's impossible to discern the losers. These special family moments, all four hundred and seventy-eight of them, are gone now and nothing's left but the photos. So we keep every one of them. Even if someone's eyes are shut. Even if our surprised looks are tired. Even if you can't tell the *Little Mermaid* doll from the niece because the picture is so out of focus.

Frustrated, we stick them in our bags, shove them in our drawers, and cram them in our boxes with all the other years of memories that will be properly organized as soon as we can be more decisive.

A few Christmases ago my brother-in-law tried to put an end to our family photo-taking madness: "Why can't you just enjoy the moment? Why does it always have to be on film?"

We all stood there staring at him blankly.

I know this for a fact. I've got a picture of it somewhere.

THE CARRY-ON
CLOSET

t's two o'clock in the morning, six hours before I
leave on my two-day business trip. There I am making the final preparations. Wearily analyzing the myriad
of potential problems I face. And arming myself with every possible solution.

Mind you, I'm not even thinking about my meet-
ings. I'm just trying to figure out what to pack.

My business partner, Mike, has apparently fared even worse than I. When we meet at the airport, all he has with him is his briefcase. Bag must be too big to carry on, I smugly think to myself as I approach him in the airport, while at the same time wondering how I'll ever be able to cram the duffel bag I'm hauling under my seat.

"You check all your stuff?" I inquire.

"What stuff?"

What stuff. That's when it hits me. He has no bag.

He has no bag, because he needs no bag. Because he's wearing an outfit that will sustain him through our entire trip. That chameleon ensemble of men's attire to which there is no equivalent in women's wear: a sport jacket, sport shirt, trousers, and a pair of loafers.

For him, it's so simple. If we go somewhere casual for dinner, he will roll up his sleeves. If it's cold out, he will wear his sport coat. And if we go somewhere nice for dinner, he will dig the necktie out of his briefcase.

And as for me? I pondered these questions at 2:30 A.M. as I stared bleary-eyed into my closet . . .

WHAT IF WE GO SOMEWHERE CASUAL FOR DINNER? If we go somewhere casual, will it be casual like jeans, a sweater, and loafers casual? Or casual like anything less than a skirt, blouse, and low heels, and I'll want to spend the night hiding in the ladies' room, casual? I stuff both versions of casual, each accompanied by the appropriate pair of shoes, into my duffel bag.

WHAT IF WE GO SOMEPLACE NICE FOR DINNER? Better throw in a dressy dress. Better throw in a dressy purse.

Better throw in a slip, pantyhose, and yes, a dressy pair of heels.

WHAT IF THE TEMPERATURE HAPPENS TO DROP TEN DEGREES? No matter how good I look, I'll be freezing, cranky, and miserable. The only rational thing to do is pack casual and dressy cool-weather alternative outfits in my bag.

Both outfits are useless without a pair of black suede boots.

WHAT IF WE'RE INVITED SOMEWHERE FORMAL? I would just like to point out that if, by chance, we are asked to a formal event while out of town, it will take him approximately 23 seconds to rent a tuxedo.

Suffice it to say, finding my ball gown and matching shoes will take slightly longer.

So here we stand at the gate. My partner, Mike, is reading his *Wall Street Journal*. And I am trying to convince the guy at the check-in that my bag really will fit under my seat.

But at least we're both ready.

That is, unless it rains . . .

If we can hit a mall between the airport and our hotel, I'll be all set.

SEVENTY-FIVE-MILE-AN-HOUR PHONE CONVERSATIONS

S eeing people on the freeway with car phones used to annoy me as much as seeing people with "Drive Carefully. Children on Board" bumper stickers. (As if the rest of us should have ones that read "No Children Aboard. Go ahead. Plow right into me.")

Who were these car phone people? And what was so important that it had to be dealt with while weaving in and out of rush hour traffic at seventy miles an hour? And when you got right down to it, wasn't the car phone really just a flimsy attempt to draw attention to the person talking on it?

All of these questions were answered when I became one of those annoying people with a car phone.

It was a purely practical purchase at the time. I had gotten a flat tire in the middle of a snowstorm, and it occurred to me that if I'd had a car phone I could've avoided risking life and limb to walk to the pay phone at the 7-Eleven that happened to be twelve feet from my car.

So, who are these car phone people? I suspect many of them, particularly women, are people like myself: people who have "sign up for auto mechanics course at the community college" right up there under "separate paper clips according to size and color" on their list of things to do. People who wear two-and-a-half-inch-high pumps in the middle of a blizzard.

This brings us to the next question: What could possibly be so important that it has to be dealt with while weaving in and out of rush hour traffic at seventy miles an hour?

Well, any number of pressing matters, really. Like, "Is there a wait at your restaurant if we go there right now?" Or, "Is your shoe sale still going on today?" Or, "Hi. Guess where I'm calling you from?" (During the initial novelty phase of owning a car phone, this last line was used on virtually every friend and family member I know until I had exhausted all of those possibilities and was to the point of randomly selecting names out of the phone book: "Hi, Mrs. Prewazniak. You don't know me, but guess where I'm calling you from? Mrs. Prewazniak? Mrs.—" CLICK)

The point is, the second you begin using a mobile phone it instantly becomes as integral to driving as your car's engine. You have information at your fingertips at a moment's notice. You expand by one more location the places where your boyfriend probably won't call you. But perhaps most important, you can break up the tedium of driving by blabbing endlessly with family and friends on subjects of no particular importance at all.

Which leads us right into question number three: Isn't a car phone really just a flimsy attempt to draw attention to the person talking on it?

Except for one incident when I almost rear-ended the woman in front of me because I was trying simultaneously to look up a number in the phone book, dial, and drive, there was only one time, without attempting to, that I drew attention to myself with regard to the phone. I wasn't using it at the time. In fact, I wasn't even in my car. No, I happened to be standing in my office the day I opened my first mobile phone bill.

Since that day, I've kept the phone locked away in the glove compartment along with the box of Wet-naps my mother sent me when I bought my new car. The phone will be used only in cases of dire emergency, such as when I have a flat tire and am stranded twelve feet away from the nearest pay phone.

Besides, I believe that when you're driving you should focus your attention on far more important things. Like putting on lipstick and trying to eat a Big Mac without getting special sauce all over the upholstery.

THE SEASONED
WORRIER

T he running joke in my family is that we could get
four flat tires, drive through a blizzard, get stuck in
a traffic jam, and still make it to the airport with three
hours to spare before the plane took off.

This is because my father was in charge of getting
us there.

A typical travel day for my family generally began at

about 6:00 A.M. with my father yelling, "Everyone in the car in five minutes! We're going to be late!"

To which my mother groggily mumbled, "The plane leaves at noon."

To which my father shrieked, "What if we get a flat?"

To which my sister groaned, "Dad, you just got all new tires. The plane leaves at noon!"

To which my father screamed, "But what if there's a traffic jam?!"

To which my other sister moaned, "Dad, we live seven minutes from the airport. The plane leaves at noon!"

To which my father bellowed, "But what if there's a blizzard?!"

To which I snapped, "Dad, it's June. It's seventy-five degrees out."

"Yes. The exact weather conditions right before the great summer blizzard of '41."

"What blizzard of '41?" I replied, but I knew I'd been defeated.

By 7:00 A.M., when it was clear to my father we'd make the plane only if a miracle occurred, we packed ourselves into the car and sped, white-knuckled, to the airport.

To save time, he dropped us at the door while he frantically searched for a parking space.

"Just go to the gate! I'll meet you at the gate!" he yelled as he peeled away.

My mom, two sisters, and I dashed in and bolted for the gate . . . The gate! . . . WHAT GATE?! There was no gate listed on the monitor for where we were going at noon.

Minutes later my dad raced in to find us standing in a puzzled stupor staring at the monitor.

"What's the hold up?" he asked.

"There's no plane leaving at noon!" we echoed in panicked unison.

"Oh. Uh, that's because it really leaves at two," my father said matter-of-factly. "I built in a little cushion time in case of an emergency."

Whew! We'd made it. And this time with only five hours to spare.

Was this any way to travel, I'd ask myself. Where was the spontaneity? Where was the thrill of sprinting down a concourse and hurling yourself onto the airplane 007 style just as the door was closing, as I'd seen so many other passengers do?

Where was the adventure of yanking open one overhead bin after the next searching for an empty while two hundred and fifty fellow passengers sat glaring?

Where was the display of athletic prowess that can only be demonstrated while trying to vault across two sets of legs and a screaming six-month-old baby to get to your seat?

Only years later, when I began traveling alone, did I have my chance to rebel. On that day I jumped into my car one hour before my flight was leaving, imagining myself sprinting down the concourse and hurling myself onto the plane 007 style, just as the doors were closing.

Ah. The smug satisfaction I would get in five short hours when I called my father from Los Angeles gloating about my adventure.

The adrenaline flowing, I turned the key in the ignition—and then proceeded to sit there for an hour and a half waiting for the tow truck to come over and give me a jump.

Naturally, I slightly altered a few of the minor details when I recounted the story of the missed flight to my father: "Yeah, it was the strangest thing, Dad. They went on strike, canceled my flight, and settled one hour later . . ."

Nor have I ever admitted to my father that in all subsequent trips I've become an exact clone of him.

"Shouldn't we get going?" I say to my partner as casually as possible the day we're flying home on our business trip.

"For crying out loud! The plane doesn't leave for three hours!" he says, checking his watch. "Relax!"

Sure, relax. I sit with him in the restaurant for what seems to be an eternity, during which I check three times to make certain I still have my ticket.

"Well, I'm relaxed and refreshed. Let's go!" I say brightly.

"Good. We now have two hours and fifty-nine minutes until the plane leaves."

Then I hear myself blurting out the words, "But what if we get a flat?"

"Have you ever gotten a flat in a cab?" he asks.

"No, but what if there's a traffic jam?"

"We're seven minutes from the airport!"

"Yes, but what if there's a blizzard?!"

"For God sakes, you're just like my father!" he snaps.

Well, it's reassuring to know my dad and I aren't the only ones who know how to travel.

AGING BY THE PHONE

I race in the front door and make a beeline for the answering machine. It's blinking. Yes. The machine is blinking. Not once, not twice, but three times. He's called. He's called to check in. I push the message button and wait for the sound of his voice—

"Hi, honey. It's Mom. Just calling to—"

Wrong voice. I push the fast forward button.

"Hi. I've got some big news. Call me."

Wrong voice again. I push the fast forward button.

"Hello. Please hold for financial advice that could change your future—"

I click off the machine. My mother has checked in with me. My best friend has checked in with me. Even a mechanical prerecorded voice has checked in with me. Everyone has checked in with me but the one person who was supposed to check in with me.

Of course I checked in with him today. I did it three times.

I checked in at 10:00 A.M. to tell him my 9:00 A.M. meeting was a disaster.

I checked in at 1:00 P.M. to tell him where I went and what I ate for lunch.

I checked in at 4:00 P.M. to tell him I was stopping at the store and wouldn't be home until 6:30.

I rewind the machine and double-check to see if perhaps I missed his check-in.

No. I've checked and rechecked and indeed he has not checked in. No matter, though. If he's going to be a little late, surely he'll check in in a while.

I rip off my business suit, throw on a pair of jeans and his favorite sweater, and redo my makeup and hair.

I check my watch. It's 7:00 P.M. I check the volume control on my phone to make sure the ringer is turned up high enough. It's on loud.

I move into the kitchen and throw together dinner: spaghetti, salad, and strawberry shortcake for dessert.

It is 8:00 P.M. Dinner is ready. I check my makeup and hair. I redo both, plus change outfits because I've splattered spaghetti sauce all over his favorite sweater.

8:15 P.M.: I sit. I wait. I alternate between checking and rechecking the spaghetti, my makeup, and my hair. I pick up the receiver and check the dial tone to make sure the phone is in working order. I try to convince myself he called to check in during the two seconds I was checking the phone.

8:30 P.M.: I'm getting annoyed. I check his office. No answer. I check his car phone. No answer. I check the spaghetti. Mmmm. Pretty good. Maybe just a few bites to tide me over until he gets home.

8:40 P.M.: WHERE IS HE? WHAT IS HE DOING? WHY DOESN'T HE CALL? We are a man and woman living in the same house. Our toiletries touch on the same shelf. Our laundry is in the same heap on the floor. We even share the same razor and blow dryer on a daily basis. This is a relationship long since graduated from the uncertain early stages where sitting and waiting and wondering intensified the excitement.

I should not now be sitting or waiting or wondering. Or for that matter, eating my second plate of spaghetti alone.

9:00 P.M.: If I didn't check in with him so often, maybe he would check in with me. I vow I will never check in with him again. I will erase his office and car phone numbers from my memory bank right after I try them both once more.

I will change out of my skintight jeans and into a sweat suit before I explode.

9:25 P.M.: The phone rings. I lunge for it.

"Hi, honey, it's Mom—"

"Mom, I'm right in the middle of something. I'll call you back."

9:35 P.M.: The phone rings again. I lunge for it.

"Hi. Guess what? I'm pregnant!"

"I'm thrilled for you! Umm, can I call you back?"

9:45 P.M.: I have alienated my own mother and my best friend, two people who cared enough to check in with me twice today. I am completely disgusted with myself for giving someone who hasn't checked in at all today priority over both. I promise myself I will refocus my energy on something other than waiting for his call.

9:50 P.M.: The strawberry shortcake is gone.

10:00 P.M.: The makeup is off. The hair is down. The contacts are out. The glasses are on.

I flop down on the couch and flip on the TV. *The Donna Reed Show* is on. Obviously Dr. Stone checked in with her. He's sitting right there with her, eating the dinner she lovingly prepared for him.

At 10:30 Ward Cleaver checks in.

At 11:00 Ricky Ricardo checks in.

They've all checked in right on time. Right on schedule. Just like clockwork.

11:31 P.M.: I wonder what it would be like to be involved with someone who checked in with me just like clockwork:

"Hi. It's me. I am going into a meeting after which I have a dental appointment after which I will call you immediately."

"Hi. Meeting went great. Teeth are bad. I am now leaving the office building to go to the bank."

"Hi. Sitting in my car waiting to use the teller machine. Just thought I'd check in . . ."

Boring. Predictable. Why would I want to know what he is doing every second of the day?

11:45 P.M.: I love the fact that he hasn't checked in. Checking in reduces a relationship to triviality. Why ever check in? Our relationship has reached such a level of interconnectedness that speaking to each other is no longer even necessary.

12:05 A.M.: I've almost talked myself into believing this when I'm overcome with worry. What if there's been some hideous accident? What if he's desperate to check in with me? What if he can't check in with me? Should I check with the police to see if there have been any hideous accidents? And what exactly do I say? "Hello. Umm. I was just checking to see if there have been any hideous—"

I hear a key in the door.

"Hi. It's me. I'm home."

Anger. Relief. Gratitude. Worry. My brain is on overdrive flipping through emotions and trying to focus on one.

"Where have you been?" I blurt out, my voice filled with all of them.

"I was at the driving range."

"It's 12:15 A.M.!"

"I know. Isn't it great? I found one that's open all night."

"Why didn't you call?" I say, my voice now shaking with anger.

"I'm sorry. I guess I lost track of the time."

"Please. Please check in with me the next time. I was so worried."

He looks at me. He can see I'm a basket case. He feels terrible. "I'm really sorry. I promise I will."

I fall asleep thinking about how lucky I am to have

someone I can become this hysterical with over not checking in with me.

Not exactly *The Donna Reed Show*. But then I believe that series was canceled before Dr. Stone ever set foot on a golf course.

LOOK WHAT THEY'VE DONE TO MY SONGS

The year was 1971. The song I knew by heart, the song I saved my allowance for two weeks to buy on a forty-five, the song I played over and over again until my mother begged me to turn it off was "It Don't Come Easy."

In the years since, I've never been able to hear it

on the oldies station without remembering when eight of my girlfriends and I stayed up all night at a slumber party creating our own "It Don't Come Easy" dance routine, and composing a fan letter to Ringo Starr.

That is, until a few years ago when a convenience store chain bought the rights to the song for their advertising campaign. Now when I dust off the old forty-five, I shut my eyes and for approximately six seconds see eight eleven-year-olds laughing and dancing wildly in the basement before a potbellied construction worker crashes our party to get a free refill on his Big Gulp.

In 1973, "Lean on Me" was the ballad blasted over the speakers in the gym the night of our first seventh-grade dance. Every time I've heard the song since then, my hands have gotten almost as clammy as they did that night two decades ago when I was invited onto the basketball court for my first slow dance.

That is, until a few years ago, when Chevrolet bought the rights. Now when I hear "Lean on Me," I shut my eyes and see my shaking, sweaty hand reaching out to his, just before a two-ton Chevy truck comes barreling through the gym, splattering mud all over my platform shoes.

My memories were dealt yet another blow last week when I turned on the TV and heard Aretha Franklin's "Rescue Me" rewritten to plug a heating and cooling company.

Horrified that I'd never be able to hear the queen of soul belt out this classic ode to romance without seeing a perspiring service man grunting and cursing his way down to the basement with a four-hundred-pound heating unit, I quickly flipped to another station. Was nothing sacred?

Apparently not. Moments later, I looked up to hear Frank Sinatra's trademark song "New York, New York." But instead of showing tantalizing images of the "news" being "spread" in the Big Apple, cream cheese was being spread on an English muffin. Wouldn't it have made more sense if they'd found a song about Philadelphia?

What next? "Bridge over Troubled Waters" for Drāno? "Lay Lady Lay" for Sealy Posturepedic?

Why do advertisers have to take all the great songs to use in their commercials? Why don't they just use only those songs we didn't like in the first place? I wouldn't care if some snack chip bought the rights to "Yummy Yummy Yummy" (I've got love in my tummy). And it wouldn't bother me a bit if a marriage counseling service licensed "I'm Henry VIII, I Am."

But having just written those words, I don't know if that's such a great idea either, as it will now be at least three weeks before I can get "I'm Henry VIII, I Am" out of my head.

That's it, then. There should be a law banning all former hit songs from being used in commercials. All offenders would be sentenced to three years of sitting in a locked room listening to "Knock Three Times" and "Watchin' Scottie Grow" over and over again, with "Sittin' on the Dock of the Bay" thrown in every once in a while for good behavior.

In the meantime, I decided to compose an angry letter to Madison Avenue:

"To whom it may concern,
     Speaking for all Baby Boomers, I wish you'd
please immediately halt the use of our favorite songs for your own sleazy ulterior motives—"

Then in the background, I heard John Lennon's
'Revolution.' I looked over to the TV to see one of my all-
time favorite songs, brilliantly juxtaposed with shots of
athletes in running shoes. It made me want to race out
and buy a pair.
     Maybe I needed to modify my letter:

"To whom it may concern,
     Speaking for all Baby Boomers, I wish you'd
please immediately halt all use of our favorite songs
for your own sleazy ulterior motives, with the exception of 'Revolution' for Nike—"

Then I heard "When a Man Loves a Woman" and
looked up to see another of my all-time favorites married
with sensual images of men and women in Levi's
jeans—
     Okay, make that two exceptions. "Revolution" for
Nike, and "When a Man Loves a Woman" for Levi's. But
that's it—"
     Suddenly "Heard It Through the Grapevine" began
to play, and I looked up to see those cute little raisins
dancing across the screen. I crumpled up my letter and
started over:

"To whom it may concern,
     If you want to use an oldies hit in one of your

commercials, please contact me first and I'll tell you if it's okay. In other words . . ."

Suddenly I couldn't help myself. I clutched my pen like a microphone and started wailing, "Don't Say Nothin' Bad About My Baby . . ."

HAVING A
BAD HAIR YEAR

'm not exactly sure why they call it a "permanent,"
but I have my own theories. The most likely being
that they're referring to the permanent state of disbelief
you find yourself in as to why you requested a hairstyle
that has made it necessary for you to stay at home with
the doors bolted and the drapes pulled shut until it
grows back out again.

Every woman knows this. We pass each other on the street, fried hair peeking out from beneath our hats. We watch our look go from bad to worse as our perms grow out, forcing kinky overprocessed hair and new bone-straight hair to intermingle on the same head.

Deep down we're all aware that the only time hair and chemicals make sense together is when the bathtub gets plugged up.

I too knew this. And yet, there I was, propelled out of my home and into the hair salon by that one brain cell that's able to reject all the facts, thinking what every woman thinks just before she gets a perm: Somehow this hairstyle will look different on me.

What intrigued me about getting a permanent was the utter simplicity of it. Unlike other self-improvements, this one required absolutely no effort on my part. No starving for six weeks on a diet for a slightly thinner me. No sweating in an exercise class for six months for a slightly firmer me.

No, this was to be an immediately noticeable change, sure to turn heads at the office. And my only challenge was deciding which magazines to read while my hairdresser completed the perm in four easy steps:

STEP ONE: Hairdresser washes hair and rolls it onto perm rods, which are pinned to head.

STEP TWO: Hairdresser squirts chemical solution out of little bottle onto head.

STEP THREE: Hairdresser sits you in chair and sets incredibly cheap-looking timer that you're sure is going to break and not go off in twenty minutes like it's supposed to and the next person to assist you will be the fire marshal arriving to put out the fire that's started on your head.

Actually, it was during this twenty-minute period that I began to fantasize about the new me that would soon exit the hair salon.

Not only would the perm greatly enhance my hair, it would reduce the size of my nose and enlarge the size of my breasts.

I envisioned my boyfriend picking me up for dinner at six that night. I would open the door and toss my head back, and say something terribly clever and flirty in the low sultry voice I was also getting with the perm. He would be so busy lunging forward to get his hands on my hair he wouldn't even hear.

We were vacationing in Paris, and he was about to surprise me with the engagement ring he had hidden in my chocolate mousse, when the timer went off, snapping me back into reality for the fourth and final step:

STEP FOUR: Hairdresser rinses you, blow-dries you, firmly reminds you not to wash your hair for at least twenty-four hours or else the perm might not hold, then spins you around in front of the mirror to give you a look at the new you.

I only wish the seven-step regimen the new me attempted to complete during the next twelve hours had been quite so simple:

STEP ONE: Race home. Jump in shower. Wash hair. Dry hair. Look in mirror. Jump back in shower. Wash hair. Dry hair. Look in mirror.

STEP TWO: Go to drugstore and buy perm relaxer. Race home. Jump in shower. Wash hair. Dry hair. Look in mirror.

STEP THREE: Cancel dinner plans with boyfriend.

STEP FOUR: Call series of girlfriends for moral support:

FRIEND ONE: Why'd you get a perm?
FRIEND TWO: I got a perm when I was fifteen. My hair all fell out.
FRIEND THREE: Why'd you get a perm?

STEP FIVE: Jump back in shower. Wash hair. Mousse hair. Gel hair. Spray hair. Dry hair. Iron hair. Pull hair back in clips. Pull hair back in bun. Root through Goodwill box and retrieve large floral scarf aunt sent from Eastern Europe.

STEP SIX: Scour closet in search of brightly colored clothing that will distract attention away from head.

STEP SEVEN: Send résumés to other cities.

Six months passed. There were pictures of me on file with a perm. Various friends and family suggested I phone them first if I ever again considered getting a perm.

But maybe I'd gotten the wrong kind of perm. This is what I couldn't help thinking after poring over such noted journals as *Hair 'n' Nail Monthly* and learning that in fact, there are many different ways in which one can have one's hair permed.

Having tried all of them, I am now quite familiar with the distinctive looks achieved by each:

TIGHT PERM: Hair turns out big frizzy mess.

SPOT PERM: Only part of hair turns out big frizzy mess.

BODY WAVE: Hair turns out big frizzy mess.

I'm happy to report that I've been perm-free for over four years now. Though I must admit that every great once in a while when I'm in the drugstore, I find myself eyeing home permanent kits, the only type of permanent I did not try.

Yes, maybe if I did it myself it would turn out differently. I try to suppress the thought. I try to remember I've already gained entrance into the Hair Disaster Hall of Fame. I don't need to win the lifetime achievement award.

$2500.00 WORTH
OF OPTIMISM

There are two kinds of people: people who can let go of things, and people who cannot.

People who can let go of things are able to accept the limitations of their talent. They know when it's time to reassess their "Thin Thighs in Thirty Days" programs. They also know when it's time to pass along the jeans that require a second party to get them off.

And then there's me. Me, who somewhere deep inside still believes that with just a few more lessons I could pass up the twelve-year-old girls in my ballet class and become a soloist with the New York City Ballet.

Me, who after 1,422 days of the program still doesn't have thin thighs, yet clings to the hope that I will not only wake up one day and have them, they'll also have grown the necessary four inches longer they would require to vaguely resemble the ones pictured on the cover of the manual.

Me, who as a result of not being able to let go of anything, has a closet stuffed with jeans in seven different sizes, one pair of which I'm actually able to wear while breathing.

And that's just the beginning of it. My closet is a microcosm of my life: all of my unwavering hope and relentless optimism, jammed into four feet of closet space on wire hangers.

I stand before it once again, determined at least in this area of my life to make some realistic judgments. Determined to consider my closet cleaning job complete only when everything in it fits my thighs and the rest of my body the size they are right now.

I start by emptying my closet and separating the clothes by category into individual piles:

CLOTHES THAT NO LONGER FIT: Includes six pairs of jeans, four pairs of leggings I forgot to take out of the dryer, and a black velvet miniskirt I bought during an endorphin surge in month eight of the "Two Weeks to a Shapelier Behind" program.

CLOTHES THAT I'VE NEVER GOTTEN AROUND TO ALTERING: Includes a black dress that needs to be lengthened, three pairs of pants that need to be shortened, and an off-white linen suit that if it were completely rebuilt would look great on me.

CLOTHES THAT HAVE NOTHING TO GO WITH THEM: Includes a navy silk skirt, an olive cotton blouse, a tweed jacket, an oversized teal angora sweater, and a floral skirt with twenty-five different colors in it, all just obscure enough so that one year and twenty-three trips to the mall later, no top or pair of shoes has surfaced that will match.

CLOTHES I NEVER SHOULD HAVE GOTTEN IN THE FIRST PLACE: Includes a hot pink minidress with a plunging neckline I bought shortly after spending a weekend alone with *Cosmopolitan* magazine, a peasant-style dress that would be perfectly wearable if I'm ever cast in a remake of *The Waltons,* and a plaid taffeta skirt with a rhinestone belt that if it weren't taffeta, weren't plaid, and didn't have rhinestones on the belt, would be stunning, but I bought it anyway because it was on triple markdown.

SHOES, BELTS, AND ACCESSORIES: Includes a pair of sienna flats I bought on the one day this year I entered a mall without bringing the legendary skirt of twenty-five colors with me, thinking they might just be odd enough to match, an assortment of scarves collected over the years, each of which has only been worn once in the store while the saleswoman was demonstrating their infinite versatility on me, and a silk flower hair ornament I bought while riding high on a Mrs. Fields sugar buzz.

That just about does it. The rejects have been plucked from my closet and are now ready to be packed away into boxes for Goodwill. I woke up. I smelled the coffee. It's time to let go, let go of it all.

And I will. Just as soon as I try on the black velvet miniskirt from my "clothes that no longer fit me" pile that I've just noticed might look great with the tweed jacket out of my "clothes that have nothing to go with them" pile. Maybe if I top the whole thing off with a festive scarf wrapped around my head, people won't even notice the velvet crease the fabric forms across the tops of my thighs.

I'm standing in front of the mirror with this getup on, thinking how wacky it looks and what a statement it would make if I could only muster the nerve to wear it out of my home, when I happen to glance over and notice the olive blouse. If I dyed it just a shade darker, then searched for a pair of shoes in the exact same shade, I could finally wear the skirt of twenty-five colors somewhere other than a dressing room in my quest for the perfect top.

Suddenly these five piles no longer represent lapses in taste, judgment, and diet, but instead are ripe with possibility.

If I lost just five more pounds, I could surely keep most of the jeans and maybe even a couple of pairs of shrunken leggings out of the reject pile.

If I would spend just one hour hemming up the

slacks in the alteration pile, I might get at least a season out of them before they're completely out of style. And even then, who's to say I'll get rid of them? I could cut them off to capri length, or better yet, shorts length to show off my long, slender thighs.

One by one every item gets hung up on wire hangers and shoved back into my closet. With each piece I promise myself I'll do whatever is necessary to make the garment work.

Last to go back into my closet is the plaid taffeta skirt with the rhinestone belt. An appropriate occasion for it will surely arise. After all, if a woman doesn't have hope, what good is closet space?

NOWHERE TO GO
BUT SIDEWAYS

June 12, 1982: I return to my office from a two-week vacation annoyed, hostile, and ready to march in to my boss and demand a huge raise.

June 12, 1989: I return to my office after a one-week vacation, during which I called in every day to make sure everyone remembers that even though I'm two thousand miles away getting snapped at in French, I still care very much about my job and my Christmas bonus package.

June 12, 1992: Forget the vacation. Ditto on the money. I return to my office from the coffee room and breathe a huge sigh of relief that I haven't been re-placed.

This is what it's come down to for most of us.

We have jobs. We're eking out a living. We aren't sitting at home in our robes and slippers wondering if our luck would change if we called the toll-free number and ordered a $400.00 set of motivational tapes.

Forget whether or not we're entirely happy. Forget whether or not we're fulfilled as human beings. Forget whether or not we think we're being paid enough. We have jobs. And if we're disgruntled, there is no shortage of people who would be happy to move in and take over our duties while we're off complaining to each other in the coffee room.

Personally, I've managed to forget the "entirely happy" part. I've managed to set aside for now the "ful-filled as a human being" part. It's the money part I'm having a little problem with.

Given the current situation at my present company, where we now have to sign out pens and pencils from the supply room, and I'm half expecting them to put twenty-five-cent coin slots on the toilet paper dispensers, you'd think I wouldn't be expecting a whole lot come raise time.

And yet there's a little part of my brain that consis-tently is able to wander off into fantasyland and convince the rest of me that this year's raise situation will be dif-ferent.

This year, when I heed my father's advice, "Just pretend you didn't get it," there will actually be some money to pretend I didn't get.

I began fantasizing about that first paycheck and all that I could buy with it approximately twenty-four hours after receiving my last raise. When I divided it into twenty-four pay periods, I could buy many things with that extra money, so long as nothing amounted to more than the price of a ham sandwich.

Because the things I'm interested in buying—such as a new house—cost slightly more than that, I was determined to give my boss no choice next raise period but to throw truckloads of money at me.

I began making a point of arriving at work an hour early every morning.

"My, you're here early," my boss would say as I nonchalantly strolled by his office (which is sort of hard to do nonchalantly because his office is on the other side of the building). I always had a huge stack of papers in my arms and walked with great purpose, as though the entire point of this mission had to do with something other than his seeing me.

"Not enough hours in the day," I'd say, my voice trailing off as I made a beeline back to my office to stare at the picture of the microwave I would buy next year with the points I had just scored with him.

But a new microwave barely scratched the surface of what I wanted to be able to buy with my next raise. And so I started working through every lunch hour.

"Don't you ever take a break?" he'd say as I nonchalantly strolled by his office at 12:30, a stack of papers in one hand, a sandwich in the other.

"Work, work, work," I'd say, speeding back to my

office to stare longingly at the magazine photo of the new range I'd surely be able to buy at this time next year.

But what were a couple lousy kitchen appliances? I wanted to be able to afford something I could really be proud of. And so I started staying every night until 8:00 P.M.

"Don't you ever go home?" my boss would say as I nonchalantly strolled by his office with a piece of pizza in one hand and a stack of papers in the other.

"You know me," I'd say, running back to my office as fast as I could to caress the tile and wood samples that would all be part of my remodeled kitchen this time next year.

As the months wore on, the amount of my fantasy raise and all the things I would buy with it continued to grow in direct proportion to my achievements and any positive reinforcement I received from my boss:

December 28: Did well in meeting. Boss congratulated me. Start shopping for couch.

February 12: Boss gives me added responsibility. Says he thinks I'm the only one who can handle it. Add drapes and coffee table to list.

May 16: Boss makes mistake of giving me an excellent performance review. Scrap kitchen remodeling project. Call realtor.

I had managed to fantasize myself up two income tax brackets on the day I nonchalantly strolled by his office and he asked me to come in and shut the door.

"I know you're due for a raise," he started, and then there was a long pause.

My heart started to race. The moment had finally come. Five minutes from now I would have my realtor on the line.

"You know things are really bad right now but—" He stopped again and stared out the window.

Yes, yes, I know. Things are really bad. Not exactly the way I had hoped he would begin his speech, but perhaps he was starting this way so that when he finished his thought, "but because of your stellar performance, I've still managed to come up with [*very large figure goes here*] for you," my ego would be boosted as well as my salary.

"But at least I don't have to make any pay cuts."

I hoped I hadn't really heard what I thought he had just said. Something about pay cuts? How was this going to segue into the part about my big raise. "Pardon?"

"I've had to put a salary freeze into effect but at least we won't have any pay cuts."

"Salary freeze?"

"I'm doing it now so I can avoid having a staff cutback."

"A what?"

"A staff cutback. You know, a layoff."

I sat there saying nothing and hanging on to the glimmer of hope that the next words out of his mouth would be "Gotcha!" and then he'd commence with his big speech about my big raise.

"Don't worry. You're doing a great job. Even if I do have to cut back, it won't affect you."

Reality was beginning to sink in. It was becoming clear to me that not only was I not getting a raise, I was going to have to continue working at my present pace just to keep my name off the cutback list.

I could think of nothing to say, and so I blurted out the words that had been programmed into me since birth by my mother. "Thanks."

"Sorry. Keep up the good work."

"Sure." I picked up my stack of papers and half-eaten danish and headed back to my office. I was back where I started a year ago, only now I was working twice as hard for the exact same amount of money.

Completely depressed, I decided to spend my lunch hour doing the only thing I could think of that would lift my spirits. I went shopping. Not for a house, or drapes, or a coffee table, or a couch, or a range, or even a microwave.

But I am the owner of a beautiful new coffee maker. I'm putting it in my office. Right next to the fold-out bed I'm having delivered next week.

MAD AS HELL AND DOING ABSOLUTELY NOTHING ABOUT IT

While my father was at work making money to support a family of five, my mother was at home all day making sure not one penny of it was misspent.

To give her two cents less change, or tell her a warranty had expired when it really hadn't, was to see my mother turn into a pit bull in a pair of flats and a sensible poly-blend suit.

There was the time she waged and won a battle against the fabric softener people because the anti-cling sheets didn't make her clothes all that fluffy and she wanted her 59¢ back.

Or the time she demanded her money back thirty-two years after her set of knives that were guaranteed to last a lifetime got dulled in the dishwasher.

Or the time she stormed the headquarters of the people who made the "childproof" china that smashed into a thousand pieces when I dropped it out our second-story window.

We're talking about a woman who has personally had a conversation with Betty Crocker over the term "moist."

She devoted herself to these causes. If it took seven hours to finally be connected to the right person at the insurance company, so what? If twelve letters were required of her to get satisfaction from the airline, big deal.

Whatever it was, she eventually would get to the bottom of it. Justice would prevail. Our family could go to sleep at night knowing that the box of Ziploc bags that neither zipped nor locked would soon be replaced by a complimentary crate of them, and most likely with a letter of apology from the company's president.

But who has time to monitor these little injustices today, I wonder. Eighty percent of Americans belong to two-income households. Most of the people I know, myself included, barely have time to get dinner on the table, let alone engage ourselves in a debate with the company over why their "lite" salad dressing has two hundred calories per tablespoon.

The second time I put on a new skirt, the hem falls out. Instead of marching back into the store and demanding they rehem it for free like I've been meaning to for the last three weeks, I find myself frantically hemming it up with duct tape a half hour before my meeting.

The blow dryer breaks one month after I buy it. Instead of shipping it back to the manufacturer along with an irate letter about how because of their inferior product, I had to simultaneously drive to the airport and attempt to dry my hair with the car heater, I find myself out of town on a week-long business trip paying double price for the same model in the hotel gift shop.

The first time I use the new bottle of antiperspirant, the little roller ball comes loose. Instead of jumping in my car and exchanging it for a new one, I spend the next month wiping excess deodorant from my underarms down to my hips, because the drugstore is ten minutes out of my way and I don't have time.

And these are only the times that the problems are obvious. What about all the times I'll never even know I've been blindly taken advantage of?

I stand at the grocery checkout watching the cashier fling my things over the bar code reader so fast, I expect to see smoke come pouring out of the register. Did it beep an extra time? Could the bar code be smeared? Could she have just charged me for two pounds of sirloin instead of a 57¢ head of lettuce? Who knows? I'm already running late, I have five bags of groceries to unpack, and I don't have time to check the receipt.

I arrive home to find a bill from my lawn service

taped to my front door: $33.00 for fertilization. Was the guy at my house an hour? Fifteen minutes? The twelve seconds it took to tape a $33.00 bill to my door? Who knows? I was off earning the money it takes to afford the luxury of being swindled by a lawn service.

I find myself filled with a constant low-level feeling that I'm being taken advantage of. Although there are those rare times, like the other day, when all the years of unaddressed little injustices boil up inside me and I'm launched into action.

"How could you?" I wrote. "I've spent three months patiently waiting for my order only to have it arrive completely wrong. I specifically asked for *six* boxes of Thin Mints and *two* Samoas! *Not* four Do-Si-Dos and three Trefoils!"

I sit in my office eating all the evidence, waiting for a response.

A PASSION FOR CARDBOARD

Of all the bizarre quirks I've inherited from my mother, I believe the one that tops the list is my inability to throw out a box.

A friend pointed this out to me the other day as she tried to help me clean out my basement.

"Why don't you just get rid of all these empty boxes?"

"Get rid of boxes?" I thought I hadn't heard her correctly.

"These big ones are taking up half your basement. Just throw them out."

"I can't. I might need them someday if I decide to move."

"You just moved in a week ago. Toss 'em."

Was she kidding? For three full weeks I'd stalked the box boy at the A & P, yanking the empties from his hands before he even knew what hit him.

I'd lurked around dumpsters in the middle of the night, directed only by my finely tuned ability to sniff out a good piece of cardboard.

I'd staked out the mailroom at my office, intercepting all perfect specimens before someone else who might be moving got their hands on them.

These weren't just boxes. They were a tribute to my most basic hunting and gathering instincts.

"Sorry," I said. "Something else will have to go."

"Well, then what about these medium-size boxes?" she asked.

"I've been saving those for when I box up stuff for Goodwill."

"You've hauled those boxes through every move for the last seven years."

"You're absolutely right. I have too much time invested in them at this point to throw them out. Any other ideas?"

She was getting exasperated. "Okay. Take that box right there, fill it with miscellaneous junk, and put it out with the garbage. That way you'll be putting it to good use and getting rid of it at the same time."

"But it's too nice a box to use for garbage. Besides, that's the box I store all my gift boxes in."

"If you'd just go to the gift wrap department, you wouldn't need to save gift boxes."

I stared at her like she was crazy. "Well, if I went to the gift wrap department, what in the world would I do with all the used gift wrap I've been collecting to use on my gift boxes?"

Shortly after that, my friend made a hasty exit, and I was left alone—to admire my collection of boxes and think about how deep the need to hang on to anything that's cardboard and has four sides runs in my family.

I thought about all of the times I've watched my mother display almost as much enthusiasm for the gift as for the box it came in.

I thought about how the women in my family will never pay retail or even wholesale for a box. No, boxes are something that by right should be as free as the air we breathe and the wire hangers we get with our dry cleaning.

I thought that someday I'll have a daughter who will learn the importance of boxes.

At the rate I'm going, she'll have a nice starter set. That is, if I can ever bear to part with them.

METROPOLITAN NIGHTMARE

"**H**ow's the house coming?"
        "Oh, it's getting there."
    This is the answer I've given to this particular question approximately three hundred and twenty-one times since I bought my house five years ago.
    My question is, when exactly will my house be "there"?

When will I be able to invite people over without prefacing entry into the master bathroom with some remark about the previous owner's taste: "Yes. Ha. Ha. He pioneered the disco movement. Ha. Ha . . . Him. Not me. Ha. Ha."

When will I be able to sit in the family room without noticing a whole new project that will sink me another twelve hundred dollars in the hole?

When will the day come when someone will ask, "How's the house coming?" and I will be able to reply, "Oh, it's there. It's there all right."

To date I've lost track of the Saturdays I've spent outside with a paintbrush or caulking gun in my hand watching happy couples wheel by on their bikes. Apartment dwellers, I sneer.

I've spent a week's vacation in my bathroom steaming off hot pink and green geometric wallpaper, and trying to decide where I'll spend my next vacation. Will it be in the kitchen stripping cabinets, or in the spare bedroom ripping up carpet?

I've run home from work and sat fuming, waiting endless hours for painters, plumbers, carpenters, and tile people to show up when they said they would. (Note: When they say they'll be there Thursday at 3:00, be sure to confirm what month and year.)

I've hired and fired. Screamed at and begged. And on those lucky days someone actually has shown up, I've raced back to work and left them there alone to finally do what they're there to do—which, from what I can tell, is eating lunch, and planning the big hunting trip they're all going to take as soon as they bill me.

But fifteen thousand dollars, three vacations, and eight contractors later, is my house "there" yet? Ha!

Every time I set my checkbook down for a breather, something new pops up. Or worse, backs up, as in the case of the recent septic tank incident, during which I was informed that it's really time to spend that five thousand dollars to hook up to the city sewer system.

Five thousand dollars? Five thousand dollars! For something you can't even see? No, thank you. For five thousand dollars I want visible results. Like recessed lighting, or a victory in court over contractor number three, who tore off the back of my house and never returned to build the addition.

I'm beginning to wonder if, should the day ever come when my house has "gotten there," I'll even know it. Or will the day pass with me standing in the family room thinking how much better it would look done in Mexican tile than the industrial carpet I laid down eight years ago when I was going through my contemporary phase?

At least I'm not alone. Everyone I know is in some stage of "getting there" with their house. Although I know finished homes must exist somewhere. The evidence exists in my inventory of home magazines with spread after spread of houses meticulously done from top to bottom, all monthly reminders of how far from "there" my own house really is.

And to add insult to injury, I find that many of these places aren't even main residences, but instead are "weekend homes." I try to imagine what it would be like to bob back and forth between two perfect homes, one of which I would occupy only for forty-eight hours a week.

But then I drift off into my favorite fantasy. The one

where the team from *Metropolitan Home* is at my house preparing for the big photo shoot. I proudly usher them through each and every room. They "oooh" at every last detail, and "ahhh" at my innate sense of style, color, and design.

"You must be a designer."

I blush. "Oh no."

The cameras start snapping away—Click. Click. Click. Click. Click. KABOOM! The massive explosion sends them all fleeing from my house to avoid the fall-out from the septic field, which has just blown up.

Suddenly I'm back in my kitchen staring out the window that needs replacing, and I realize that my house is *there. There,* down the street with a "For Sale" sign in front. With just a little coat of paint and some landscaping, it could be perfect.

THE FINE ART OF MISCOMMUNICATION

'm convinced we'd have a new bestseller if someone published an instruction manual for men entitled *What You're Supposed to Say When She Shamelessly Begs You for a Compliment.*

If there were such a handy manual, I'd never again have to have the following conversation:

ME: How do you like my hair?

HIM: (AFTER A LONG PAUSE) It looks nice.

ME: What's wrong with my hair?!

HIM: Nothing. There's nothing wrong with it.

ME: But you paused like there might have been something wrong with it.

HIM: I was admiring it. And then I said it looked nice.

ME: Just nice?

HIM: It looks great! I think your hair looks great! Okay? Now are you happy?!

ME: No. Because it wasn't spontaneous. Therefore the entire compliment is completely irrelevant.

Furthermore, if there were such a manual, I would never have *this* conversation again:

ME: Do you think I look fat?

HIM: No. Not at all.

ME: You do. You think I look fat.

HIM: I just said you don't look fat.

ME: Yes. But you didn't say I look thin. Therefore you must think I'm somewhere in the fat to mid-fat range.

I realize that in both conversations I wasn't just begging for a compliment. I wanted to hear a specific set of words, spoken with a particular inflection, an exact facial expression, and body language that I'd pre-scripted in my head.

How was he supposed to know that upon seeing my fried, permed hair for the first time, the conversation was supposed to go like this:

FANTASY ME: How do you like my hair?

FANTASY HIM: (DROPPING THE SPORTS SECTION, HIS EYES WIDENING) Your hair looks beautiful, yet no more beautiful than it has ever looked in the 3,465 other days that I've known you.

FANTASY ME: Really?

FANTASY HIM: (LEAPING UP AND LUNGING TOWARD ME) Yes! Yes! I must run my fingers through it this very minute!

FANTASY ME: It feels like a Brillo pad.

FANTASY HIM: (HANDS PLANTED IN MY HAIR) No, it feels soft and sexy. Even if it did feel like a Brillo pad as you suggested, which it does not, mind you, I've always loved the way a Brillo pad feels against my skin.

Or, how was he supposed to know that as I stood before the mirror, a fistful of upper thigh fat in each hand, the conversation I wanted to have was this one:

FANTASY ME: Do you think I look fat?

FANTASY HIM: (A LOOK OF UTTER CONFUSION ON HIS FACE AS THOUGH HE HASN'T HEARD ME CORRECTLY) Fat?

FANTASY ME: Yes, fat.

FANTASY HIM: (LOUD BURST OF LAUGHTER) Whew! That's a good one. I thought you were going to say, "Do I look too thin?" to which I would have responded, "Yes, you could stand to gain a few." But too fat? (ANOTHER SPONTANEOUS BURST OF LAUGHTER) Oh, you just slay me sometimes . . .

FANTASY ME: Really?

FANTASY HIM: Yes. We must grab our coats and go buy you a gallon of ice cream right now.

Of course, neither of these situations, real or imagined, even begins to compare to the following one, in which not only did he not know what I expected him to say, he had no idea what I was talking about in the first place:

ME: Well, what do you think?
HIM: (TENTATIVELY) Your hair looks beautiful?
ME: No.
HIM: (MEEKLY) You look incredibly thin?
ME: Wrong again.
HIM: Give me a hint.
ME: The living room. I bought a rug, rearranged the furniture, and hung a twelve-foot painting on the wall.
HIM: Oh. (AFTER A LONG PAUSE) It looks nice.
ME: What's wrong with the living room?
HIM: Nothing. There's nothing wrong with the living room.
ME: But you paused like there might have been something wrong with it.

(You can guess how the rest of this conversation goes.)

In retrospect, I realize that unless he had been looking very closely and happened to notice that I'd bought a rug, rearranged the furniture, and hung a twelve-foot painting on the wall, my question, "Well, what do you think?" could have pertained to any number of things.

All the more reason men need this potential bestseller. It would give step-by-step instructions about what to do when faced with every possible situation:

> She has just asked you what you think. You have no idea whether she's searching for a response pertaining to her hair, attire, accessories, weight, spark plugs she just bought, or the status of your relationship.
>
> Without skipping a beat, you must confidently look her in the eye and say, "Terrific."
>
> Note that this will not be a sufficient answer, as she will probably now ask you the question, "Really?"
>
> Again, you must give no indication that you haven't the foggiest idea what she is talking about. Answer: "Yes. Incredible! And I really mean that!"
>
> At this point she may get more specific: "Do you like the color?"
>
> Unless you are altogether sure that she is referring to her hair, lipstick, attire, or furniture, we recommend you remain completely vague: "Yes. I love it! An outstanding choice!"
>
> Then, as quickly as possible, change the subject. Something like, "You look so thin. Let's go buy a cheesecake," is preferable.

But beyond these suggestions, the manual would give proposed responses when the man is sure, beyond a doubt, what the woman is talking about.

Some sample replies:

"Heavens, no. Madonna's thighs look flabby compared to yours."

"I don't see any wrinkles around your eyes."

"A blemish? Where?"

"No. It's not rubbery. I really like my steak well done."

"The way your earrings pick up the muted greenish-gray fleck in your tweed jacket is really amazing."

"You're so much better-looking than Michelle Pfeiffer."

"Where are the *Sports Illustrated* swimsuit photographers when you need them?"

I was about to run this concept by my sweetheart the other day. But he was preoccupied with something else.

"Do you think I'm going bald?" he asked.

I paused, studying the top of his head for a few moments, and then replied, "No, not at all."

"You do! You think I'm going bald!"

"I just said you *weren't* going bald."

"But you paused like you were thinking I'm going bald . . ."

Come to think of it, women will need a similar text.

PONDERING LIFE AND THE
TOILET CLEANER COMMERCIAL

They say that advertising is supposed to imitate life. Whose life? That's what I wondered the other night when the commercial for the tile cleaner came on.

It featured a housewife straight out of *The Stepford Wives,* standing in the bathroom next to the toilet, lamenting the trials and tribulations of having to clean up after her husband and sons. Meaning: They apparently go to the toilet everywhere in the bathroom except for the toilet.

I waited for the Energizer rabbit to come hopping through and save the day. He didn't. I waited for the moment at the end of the commercial when she would stick their heads in the toilet and give them swirlys. She didn't.

Completely disgusted, I grabbed the remote, zapped them off, and picked up a magazine. The first ad I ran across was for a clothing manufacturer, and it featured a priest and nun kissing. No sweaters. No blouses. No skirts. No pants. Just a priest and nun kissing.

I searched the page for the Energizer rabbit. He wasn't there. I turned the page looking for the fashion update article breaking the bad news that the vestment look is in. Thankfully, it wasn't there, either.

It was suddenly so clear to me. There are two basic life-style categories advertisers are trying to tap into.

First, there are the "WHO WE WERE" ads, which feature people and situations about as subtle as a '52 Chevy truck. They harken back to a simpler time when people actually knew what they wanted and said what they meant.

When a man saw a woman who took his fancy, he told her so, and asked her out on a date. When he fell in love with her, he asked her to get married. When they got married, the happy couple moved into a house with a white picket fence, and gave birth to little boys who went to the toilet everywhere except for the toilet, and little girls who scurried around with the lady of the house cleaning up after them.

On the other end of the spectrum are the "WHO WE ARE" ads. Ads that are so subtle, you wonder if the people who thought them up even know what they mean. Car ads with no cars. Perfume ads with no perfume. Blue jean ads with no blue jeans.

But then, as vague and confused as these ads may seem, I suppose they're no more so than the generation they're trying to reach: a generation that hasn't the foggiest idea of what we want for ourselves, let alone from each other.

When a man sees a woman he wants to take out, he spends his next four therapy sessions figuring out if he's really ready for another relationship. When they think they like each other, they spend five months in individual therapy, deciding if moving in together is really the right thing to do. When they move in together, they wind up in joint therapy analyzing whether or not his missing the toilet and hitting the wall is in some way reflective of his feelings about the relationship.

But I'm tired of pondering the world of advertising and what it all means. I flip the TV back on just in time to catch a commercial for a bran cereal. It features a woman who has Barbie measurements, three perfect children, an adoring husband, and a major court case she's about to run off and try, as soon as she finishes cheerfully making sure her loving family has gotten its fiber intake for the day.

Ah. "WHEN PIGS LEARN TO FLY": A whole new category to consider.

UNDERWEAR
FROM HELL

There are two times in a woman's life when she
should under no circumstances enter the lingerie
department: a) When she's feeling bad about herself.
And b) When she's feeling good about herself.

When I'm feeling bad about myself, I wake up feeling a little heavy. What a perfect day to buy some pretty

underthings, I think. It'll make me feel better about myself. And besides, I'm down to three pairs of briefs and one bra that aren't in shreds.

I enter the lingerie fitting room with eight bra and French cut bikini sets, a beautiful floral patterned camisole and tap pant number, and a lace body stocking, ready to be transformed into a Victoria's Secret model.

I hook myself in and spin around for a look in the mirror. The tap pants make my legs look short and fat. The French cut panties make my legs look long and fat. The bras can barely fasten in the back, yet the cups sit half-empty in front. And the body stocking that looked so beautiful on the hanger makes me feel like a sausage stuffed into a nylon casing.

Grimly I make my way back out to the floor for more lingerie. Grimly I make my way back to a new dressing room with mirrors that won't make me look so short and squatty. Minutes later I'm back out. Minutes later I'm back in. Out. In. Out. In. Out. In. Out. In.

I stand in the dressing room with a mountain of lingerie heaped on the floor, a monument to my atypical body type.

I curse a lingerie industry that's managed to create a bra to fit every woman's breasts but my own.

I curse the department store that's equipped every fitting room in the lingerie department with cheap substandard mirrors that make their customers look short and squatty.

I curse the security personnel who I'm sure have been called in from every department to monitor what's going on in fitting room three.

On trip number six I happen to glance in the fitting room next to me and see an eighteen-year-old in the hip-hugger and bra set I'd just flung on the floor.

The elastic on her panties cuts no path across the bottom third of her behind. The bra forms perfectly around her breasts with no wrinkles or puckers of nylon. And not that I was looking that closely but I did happen to notice, before she yanked the curtain shut, that the bra was on the first hook instead of the third with no rolls of fat bulging out on top or bottom of the elastic band.

That does it. Without trying another thing on, I march out, pondering what it will be like to spend the next thirty-five years of my life in the same three pairs of underpants and one bra.

On the way out I hit the shoe department. I may not have the body of an eighteen-year-old, but I do have the feet. I leave the store, arms loaded down with shoes to prove it.

The only thing worse than shopping for lingerie when a woman is feeling bad about herself is shopping for lingerie when she feels good about herself.

On that day, I wake up feeling thin. What a great day to hit the lingerie department, I think to myself. I feel great about myself and some nice new pretty underthings will make me feel even better. Besides, I'm down to three pairs of underpants and a bra that aren't completely in shreds.

My first trip into the dressing room has me in a pair of sensible white high-tops and bra my mother had recommended. I'm even thinner than I thought, I tell myself, looking in the mirror. Maybe I can go with something a little more revealing . . .

Trip number two brings me back to the dressing room with slightly racier lingerie: pretty lacy bras, French cut bikini bottoms, and heck, why not give that cute little floral tap pant and camisole number a whirl?

The third trip has me outfitted to do a road tour with Madonna, and I'm sure the security personnel would agree if they weren't so busy wiping steam away from their monitors.

Minutes later I exit the fitting room with virtually everything I tried on except for the sensible white high-tops and bra my mother recommended.

I peel out of the mall parking lot, making a brief stop at the McDonald's drive-through on the way home, because who has time to sit down and wait for a salad and soup when I've got all this beautiful underwear.

Twelve minutes later I'm home, trying on my new wardrobe and wondering what that special someone will think tonight when the saucy new me is unveiled.

He'll think I look like a tramp. And a short squatty one at that, I think, getting a load of myself in the mirror, sporting what fifteen minutes ago were the tap pants and matching camisole in which I felt so confident.

Could a Big Mac and fries have completely changed my body type in twelve minutes flat? Or is that cut-rate department store to blame with their cheap, substandard mirrors that made me appear thinner than I really am?

One by one the outfits come on and off. One by one they go back in the shopping bag.

It's 6:15. Plenty of time to hit the shoe department.

GUS, CUPID, AND FEBRUARY 14

I sometimes wonder if someone came up with a new spokesperson for Valentine's Day, it might generate a little more interest and enthusiasm from men.

After all, most of the guys I know have never really taken to Cupid, a little man who likes to wear pink tights and play the lute when he's not flitting about shooting arrows at the general population.

Maybe if Cupid were missing a few teeth in front and shot heart-shaped hockey pucks at unsuspecting passersby, men would sit up and take notice.

Maybe if word got out that on his time off he wrestled cattle or hung out on an oil barge, he could bond with the guys.

Maybe if his name were changed to something slightly more macho like Duke or Gus, the occasion he represents would gain some manly respect.

Maybe then guys would think, "Hey, this Gus guy's all right. He's obviously macho, and yet come Valentine's Day, he has no trouble running away with his emotions."

Of course, women have no trouble with the concept of running away with their emotions on Valentine's Day. "WHAT DO YOU MEAN YOU DIDN'T GET ME ANYTHING?!! . . . HOW COULD YOU NOT KNOW?!! THERE HAVE BEEN ADS ON TV, ADS ON RADIO, ADS IN NEWSPAPERS AND DISPLAYS IN EVERY STORE SINCE DECEMBER 26TH!!!"

The problem seems to be that the very things that drive men away from Valentine's Day in droves—things like wild, unbridled romance, public displays of affection, verbal declarations of undying love (basically the chance for the relationship to be everything it hasn't been for the last three hundred and sixty-four days), are the same ones that drive women to it like a two-for-one shoe sale.

Women fixate on Valentine's Day. We spend weeks scouring malls and specialty shops and mail order catalogues for the perfect gift. We spend countless lunch hours searching for just the right card. And when every retailer and card manufacturer in America fails us, we go about making just the right gift and card in the wee hours of the night and behind closed office doors during the day.

All the while, we fantasize about what this Valentine's Day will be like. So, no matter what the man does, it's doomed to fall short of the perfect fairy tale we've woven in our heads at 2:00 A.M. while half delirious and finishing up our thoughtful, meaningful gifts.

FANTASY VALENTINE'S DAY SCENARIO

Man shows up at door with large bouquet of your favorite kind of flowers. He presents you with some thoughtful gift only the two of you could understand, such as the subway token from your first date embedded with diamonds and hanging on a gold chain. After telling you how particularly beautiful you look on this Valentine's night, he whisks you away to your favorite restaurant for a candlelight dinner. Your hands touch. Your feet touch. You gaze into each other's eyes. Suddenly the passion is so great that you both must exit the restaurant before you've even finished your calamari appetizers so as not to cause a scene.

REAL-LIFE VALENTINE'S DAY SCENARIO

THE WOMAN AT 5:15 P.M., FEBRUARY 14: Sits behind closed office door finishing card she's made and wondering what special romantic surprise the man has planned for the evening.

THE MAN AT 5:15 P.M., FEBRUARY 14: Calls buddy to see what he's doing tonight. Buddy says that he just found out from his buddy who found out from his buddy who found out from his girlfriend who's no longer speaking to him that today is Valentine's Day.

THE WOMAN AT 5:16 P.M., FEBRUARY 14: Compares finished card to two other handmade cards, trying to decide which one is better. Wonders if she should just keep all three in her pocketbook and present the one or two most appropriate depending on his gift.

THE MAN AT 5:16 P.M., FEBRUARY 14: Gets on phone and begins frantically calling every restaurant in town in search of one lousy dinner reservation for two.

THE WOMAN AT 5:30 P.M., FEBRUARY 14: Wonders what he meant when he just called and said he'd be over in an hour but had to stop and do a few things. Things . . . like picking up the subway token he's had embedded with diamonds at the jewelry store? Is that what he meant? . . .

THE MAN AT 5:30 P.M., FEBRUARY 14: Bolts out of office and gets in line with every other man in city at florist.

THE WOMAN AT 6:30 P.M., FEBRUARY 14: Stands in stupor in bedroom trying to decide what to wear, and which cards and gifts to give.

THE MAN AT 6:30 P.M., FEBRUARY 14: "What do you mean, all you have left are green-tipped carnations?!"

THE WOMAN AT 6:35 P.M., FEBRUARY 14: "I know he'd love it if I gave him this shirt because it's just like the one he wore on our first date. But then this scrapbook with ticket stubs and matchbooks and photos of everything we've done together this year is so sentimental . . ."

THE MAN AT 6:35 P.M., FEBRUARY 14: Stops at drugstore and grabs Whitman's Sampler and only Valentine's Day card he can find.

THE WOMAN AT 6:37 P.M., FEBRUARY 14: Changes for the third time, this time into a black cocktail dress, and searches for a handbag large enough to accommodate all gifts and cards.

THE MAN AT 6:37 P.M., FEBRUARY 14: Sits in parking lot inking out words on card that don't apply to situation, such as "To my beloved mother from her devoted son," and tries to rewrite to apply to relationship with girlfriend.

THE WOMAN AT 6:45 P.M., FEBRUARY 14: "The golf booties with little hearts I knitted for him are really the perfect gift."

THE MAN AT 6:45 P.M., FEBRUARY 14: "Nix the card. I'm fifteen minutes late."

THE WOMAN AT 6:48 P.M., FEBRUARY 14: Answers door and attempts to graciously accept green-tipped carnations and Whitman's Sampler, knowing that so much more lies ahead tonight. Then asks if maybe she should call the restaurant to tell them they're going to be running a little late.

THE MAN AT 6:48 P.M., FEBRUARY 14: "Where we're going, they don't take reservations."

THE WOMAN AT 6:49 P.M., FEBRUARY 14: Thinks to herself how a privately catered dinner at his house surpassed even her wildest expectations.

7:00 P.M., FEBRUARY 14: Relationship ends in the parking lot at Denny's Restaurant.

THE MAN AT 7:15 P.M., FEBRUARY 14: Calls up his buddy to see what's going on tonight.

THE WOMAN AT 7:15 P.M., FEBRUARY 14: Sits punching holes in the bottoms of Whitman's Samplers in search of caramels while trying to figure out how to make golf booties into a sweater for herself.

If my new Cupid spokesman idea took off, this whole typical Valentine's Day scenario would have turned out differently. Heart-shaped-puck-shooting Gus would have inspired the man to spend three weeks searching the city for the perfect, thoughtful gift. The man would have stayed up half the night obsessing over his romantic handmade card. Then come February 14, he would let out all of his pent-up emotion: "WHAT DO YOU MEAN, YOU DIDN'T GET ME ANYTHING?!!!"

Hey, I never said that a guy named Gus who's missing two front teeth and wastes his time hanging out on an oil barge would go over big with women.

INCHING INTO MY MOTHER'S ARMS

OCTOBER 5, 10:15 P.M.

"What time does your flight get in?"
    "7:08 P.M."
"Daddy and I will be waiting for you."
"Mom, please, I'll get a cab to your house."

"And not be there to see our baby get off the plane?"

"Mom, I'm thirty-two years old. I'm perfectly capable of getting a cab."

"We'll see you at 7:08."

"I'm taking a cab."

"But, sweetie—"

"Mu-thrrrr—"

"If that's what you really want."

"Really. Love you, Mom. Bye."

Fifteen hundred miles away from her house, and the battle of wills has already begun. I am a grown woman, with a grown-up career that carries me 40,000 frequent flier miles every year and requires me to hail cabs and, yes, sometimes even get hopelessly lost in rental cars in strange cities all by myself.

To my mother I am ten years old. I am, was, and will always be frozen in time with pigtails and freckles, and an escort walking me off the plane if, God forbid, she wasn't on the flight with me.

Now the only remaining glimmer of youth on my face is a persistent case of acne vying for the same space as my emerging wrinkles.

I can take care of myself. I do it every day of my life, fifteen hundred miles away from her. I want her to understand that.

OCTOBER 6, 7:00 P.M.

I get off the plane, shoulders aching from the weight of fifty pounds of carry-on luggage, and drag my way to the waiting area.

Husbands are greeting wives. Wives are greeting husbands. Grandparents are reunited with squealing grandchildren. Boyfriends and girlfriends. Sisters and brothers. Parents and grown-up children who obviously have found cheaper ways to exert their independence than with $25.00 cab fares.

I stop for a moment, checking faces to see if maybe my parents decided to surprise me.

They're not there. But after all, I wanted it this way.

I sit in the cab resting my shoulders, watching the meter tick away, and waiting to have our reunion and week-long visit at their house on my own terms.

OCTOBER 6, 8:30 P.M.

"Dinner's ready! I made your favorite. Pot roast."

"Thanks, Mom. But I'm really trying to cut down on meat. I'll just have a salad."

"But it's your favorite."

"Salad, please."

"I'm having some. See?" She takes a bite.

"I don't want any."

"Mmmmm. It's really good."

"Hope you enjoy it."

The truth is, I do want some. I'm dying for some. My mother's pot roast is not to be believed. I've watched her make it dozens of times. I have her recipe. She's talked me through her recipe fifteen hundred miles away over the phone. She's all but put the pot roast in the oven for me. And yet somehow when I make it, it always turns out like a piece of rubber.

Had I not just made such a big deal over not wanting any, I might now be enjoying a pleasant conversation with my mother instead of fixating on the platter of meat and potatoes and carrots and onions in front of me, and wondering when I can grab a piece without her seeing me.

It would make her so happy if I would just give in and take a piece. But I can't. I won't. I am a thriving, productive member of society who has learned to function on a day-to-day basis without pot roast, and she must understand that tonight will be no different.

I go to bed starving, the lingering smell of pot roast taunting me as I try to fall asleep.

OCTOBER 7, 1:00 A.M.

I tiptoe out of my bedroom, one hallway and one flight of stairs away from the pot roast. Quietly, ever so quietly past my parents' bedroom door and down the—

"Do you need something?" my mom says, springing from the bedroom.

"No, I'm fine. I just wanted another blanket."

"You're cold? I'll get you a comforter—"

"Mom—"

"I'll turn up the heat—"

"Mom—"

"I'll set the space heater up in your room."

"Mom—"

"Here, take my electric blanket. I don't need a blanket. I don't like blankets. All I really need is a sheet . . . unless you want that, too."

"Thanks, Mom."

I go back to bed, the heat set at eight-five, a space heater at my side, and every blanket in her house on top of me.

Maybe if my head is buried under the weight of seven blankets I won't be able to smell the pot roast.

OCTOBER 7, 7:30 A.M.

"Waffles for breakfast?"

"I'll just have some coffee."

"How about a nice bowl of oatmeal?"

"No. I'd like some coffee."

"A piece of toast?"

"Coffee."

"Fruit?"

"Coffee!"

"A little glass of orange juice?"

"Mom!"

"Okay, okay, coffee."

Another victory. My stomach grumbles loudly in protest.

OCTOBER 7, 11:30 A.M.

"Have any laundry? I'm doing a load."

"That's okay, Mom. I'll do my stuff later."

"Don't be silly. I'll just throw your stuff in with Dad's and mine."

"I can handle it, Mom."

"It's no trouble really."

I turn back to reading the paper without responding. I do have a few things to wash. No, actually everything I brought with me is filthy because I didn't have time to do the laundry before I left.

Two hours later, when I finally feel like washing my clothes, my mother suggests we go shopping.

I spend the afternoon at the mall with her, exerting my independence in a wrinkled pair of pants and a blouse with a coffee stain on the collar.

OCTOBER 8, 7:00 A.M.

I wake up freezing and exhausted and starving and miserable. At two o'clock in the morning I got within fifteen feet of the pot roast before the light flicked on and my mother asked me if I needed anything. I told her I was too hot and well, suffice it to say, the air conditioner was immediately flipped on, and now it must be fifty-seven degrees in here.

I lie in bed thinking about what I've proven to my mother in the last thirty-six hours. That I'm stubborn? That I'm belligerent? That I'm as obstinate as I was when I was ten years old and flung myself into her arms when I was escorted off the plane, but then refused to let her help me with my Barbie case and purse because I was big enough to carry them all by myself? Is that what I've proven?

Impressive. Very impressive.

In four days I'll be fifteen hundred miles away from her. I'll be immersed in my own grown-up life and my own grown-up career and getting lost in rental cars in strange cities. There will be no one to take care of me.

I'll be stuck fending for myself, standing over the kitchen sink with a bowl of cereal for dinner and nothing to wear tomorrow because I haven't made my monthly pilgrimage to the laundry room.

I'm starving and cold and disgusted with myself. I want my mother. No, let me put that another way. I want my mommy. I want her to do all the things she's been desperate to do for me. I want her to take care of me. I want to be treated like the ten-year-old I've been acting like since I got here two days ago.

I jump out of bed, throw on a filthy shirt and wrinkled pair of pants, and race down to the kitchen.

"What's for breakfast?"

"Nothing. My daughter doesn't eat food."

"I'm kind of hungry, Mom."

"You are?" I nod my head and I can see her eyes lighting up. "How about some waffles?"

"Great."

"Sausage?"

"Yes."

"Orange juice?"

"Yeah, Mom, it all sounds great."

The smell of batter and maple syrup and sausage fills the room.

There are only four days until I have to go home and take care of myself.

So much pot roast in my future. So little time.